JET Engine

Turbines

Conforti, Facundo
/ Facundo Conforti. - 1a ed. - Mar del Plata : Facundo Jorge Conforti,
2023.
194 p. ; 21 x 15 cm.

1. Aviación. I. TÌtulo.
CDD 629.1343

1ra Edición.

Introduction

The transition from piston engines to jet engines is often a significant milestone in every pilot's career.

Turbines or jet engines offer different performance characteristics compared to piston engines. Not only do turbines deliver superior power, but they also enable flight at much higher altitudes than piston engines.

In this work, you will learn all the basic operating principles of a turbine, along with the main components that make up these types of engines, and a step-by-step guide on transitioning from one engine type to another.

Capt. Facundo Conforti

Main

Chapter 1 – Jet engine system

Chapter 2 – jet engine associated systems

Chapter 3 – Fuel system

Chapter 4 – Engines of Airbus A320 and Boeing B737

Chapter 5 – Jet engine performance

Chapter 1

Jet engine system

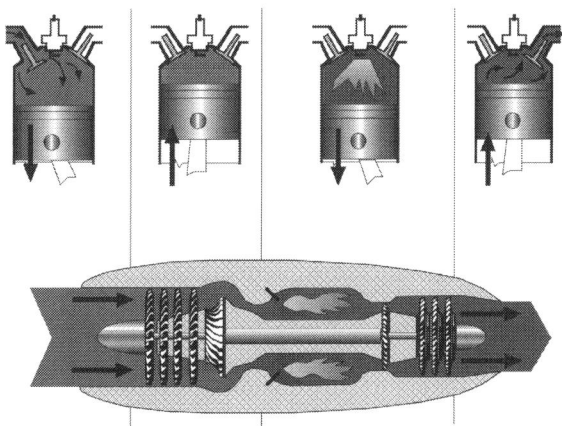

Basic principles

Physics defines propulsion as the action or movement generated by a specific force that pushes or impels something forward. More precisely, in aviation, it is the force that pushes the aircraft, providing it with speed to generate lift.

Aircraft are powered by two different types of engines, which correspond to two principles of thermodynamics. Although there are variations, as shown in the following diagram, the operating principles are fundamentally two.

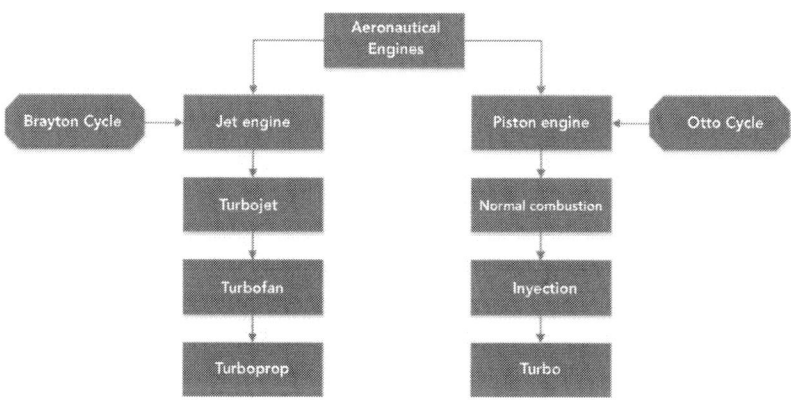

Reciprocating engines used in aviation have over a century of development. From the first flight of the Wright brothers to the present day, they have evolved and advanced in reliability alongside their development. Jet engines utilize the principles of Newton's laws of physics and the Brayton thermodynamic cycle to generate thrust. Among the most commonly used jet engines in aviation, we find the following:

• **Turbojet**: This was the first type of jet engine developed, equipping various types of aircraft (both civil and military). It originated in 1930 in Germany. The engine consists of an air intake system, a compressor stage, a combustion stage, and a turbine stage driven by exhaust gases. This operation generates the thrust that propels the aircraft. A typical example of this type of engine is the Pratt & Whitney JT3D, which powered aircraft like the Boeing 707, Douglas DC-8, and Boeing B-52, among others.

• **Turbofan**: This is an evolution of the turbojet. While it operates on the same basic principle, these engines have dual stages of compression and gas expansion. It is also noteworthy that combustion in the chambers occurs with only a portion of the air entering the engine; the remaining air bypasses the core and mixes with the exhaust gases to form the total thrust. This type of engine is the most commonly used in large aircraft today. A typical example is the Rolls-Royce Trent series, which in its various versions, powers aircraft from the Boeing 757 and MD-11 to the modern Boeing 787 Dreamliner (Trent 1000 version).

• **Turboprop**: This type of engine revolutionized aviation. It is a jet engine that, instead of producing thrust through exhaust gases, generates mechanical work that drives a shaft. This shaft turns a reduction gearbox that drives the propeller. This type of propulsion is most commonly used in medium-sized aircraft for transport and training. The most prominent example of this engine is the Pratt & Whitney PT6, a turboprop that powers aircraft ranging from the Air Tractor AT-600 crop duster to the multipurpose transport aircraft like the Cessna 208 Grand Caravan.

• **Turboshaft**: This is essentially a turboprop engine adapted to drive the transmission systems of helicopters. A clear example is the Turbomeca Arriel engine, which in its various variants powers helicopters such as the Eurocopter AS 350 B2 and AS 350 B3.

In this book, we will focus on the operating principles, components, characteristics, and protection of reciprocating (or piston) engines, the propulsion used in the majority of light general aviation aircraft. Therefore, we will begin by explaining the fundamental principle of the reciprocating engine... the Otto Cycle.

What is the Otto Cycle?

Before answering this question, we must understand a key concept: thermodynamics. It is the branch of physics that studies the interaction between temperature and the various manifestations of energy, encompassing all processes involving these variables. With that in mind, let's delve into the Otto Cycle.

The Otto Cycle is a thermodynamic cycle that describes the fundamental physical principle of operation for internal combustion engines (reciprocating engines in aviation). This cycle was discovered in 1876 by the German engineer Nicolaus Otto (1832-1891), who later applied it in the invention of the first internal combustion engine.

This thermodynamic principle governs both two-stroke and four-stroke internal combustion engines, with diesel engines falling under the category of four-stroke engines. For the purposes of this book, we will focus on the four-stroke cycle, which is used in reciprocating engines in aviation.

The Otto Cycle for four-stroke engines consists of four stages or strokes: intake, compression, combustion, and exhaust. The following diagram illustrates how these four strokes occur within the cylinder, piston, and crankshaft assembly.

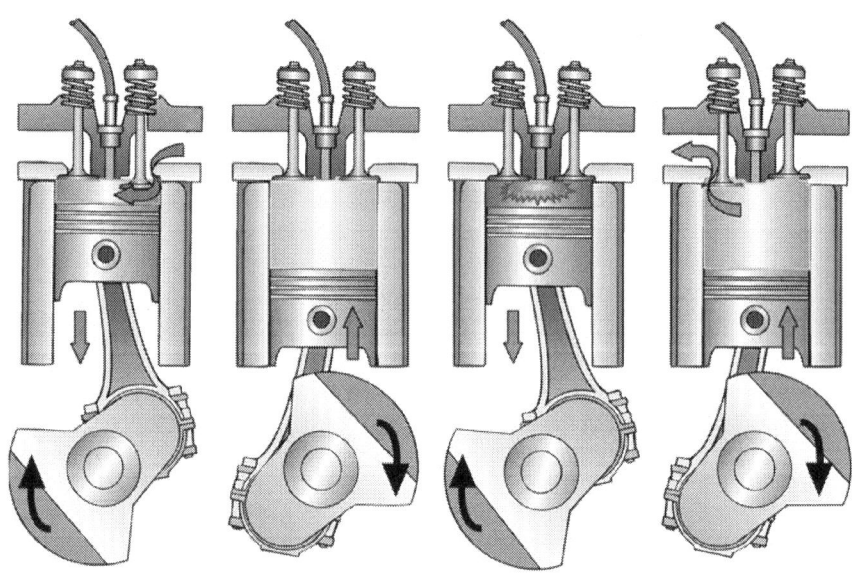

The four strokes observed in the previous figure encompass the sequential process that occurs within each cylinder of the engine. The work generated by each piston drives the crankshaft, which subsequently rotates the propeller, thereby creating the aerodynamic effect that provides the final propulsion for the aircraft. Let's delve into how this phenomenon occurs in detail.

The principle of the engine's four strokes occurs in a single revolution or RPM. In other words, during one complete rotation of the crankshaft, the following four steps take place:

Intake

When the intake valve of the cylinder opens, while the exhaust valve remains closed, a mass of air enters the cylinder chamber. This phenomenon is due to the suction effect created by the piston during its downward stroke towards bottom dead center. The piston acts like a plunger that draws in air during this stroke. By the time the connecting rod and piston reach bottom dead center, the necessary amount of air for combustion has entered the cylinder.

The downward movement of the piston is driven by the connecting rod, which is integral with the crankshaft. The crankshaft is precisely responsible for coordinating the movement of all connecting rods and pistons within each cylinder in a sequential and harmonized manner.

Compression

After reaching bottom dead center, the connecting rod and piston begin their upward stroke towards top dead center. When the piston reaches bottom dead center, the intake valve closes, creating a sealed chamber within the cylinder.

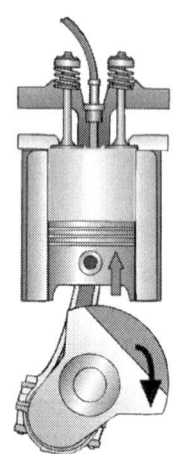

As the piston travels upwards along the cylinder walls, the contained air is compressed. When the piston reaches top dead center, the air mass is at its maximum compression. The connecting rod and piston maintain this position for a fraction of a second until the next phase begins.

Combustion

With the cylinder chamber filled with compressed air and both valves closed, fuel enters and then the spark plug ignites. The spark from the spark plug causes the vaporized fuel, along with the air mass inside the cylinder, to ignite suddenly, resulting in a controlled explosion. The combustion of the fuel, like any explosion, releases a significant amount of energy in the form of heat and pressure. The sudden increase in pressure in the chamber drives the piston (piston and connecting rod assembly) towards bottom dead center, marking the

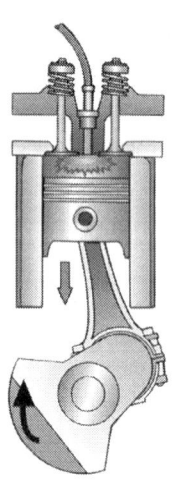

beginning of the fourth stage of the cycle. Once combustion occurs, the exhaust valve opens to allow the combustion by-products to exit through the exhaust.

Expansion

The pressure contained in the chamber after combustion causes an expansion effect that literally pushes the piston (piston and connecting rod assembly) towards top dead center. The energy from the expansion of combustion is converted into mechanical work that is transmitted through the connecting rod to the crankshaft.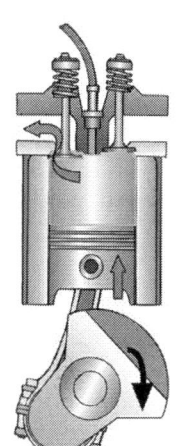

With the exhaust valve closed during the final phase of expansion, the intake valve opens again to initiate the intake stroke of the next cycle.

The four strokes described in the preceding paragraphs occur sequentially in each cylinder of the engine. The mechanical work transmitted to the crankshaft by each cylinder assembly determines the force and speed at which the crankshaft rotates. In other words, the energy produced by each cylinder assembly and the sequence of the process translate into revolutions per minute (RPM) and horsepower (hp) or kilowatts (kW).

The Otto Cycle, in theory, is an ideal adiabatic thermodynamic cycle. However, in practice, the transformations occurring in the cylinder chamber do not occur at constant volume. Therefore, the Otto Cycle remains a theoretical expression serving as the foundation for the physical principle governing internal combustion engines.

The efficiency of the engine depends on the compression ratio. This ratio represents the maximum volume available in the sealed cylinder chamber, delimited between top dead center and bottom dead center. The compression ratio dictates the type of gasoline (octane rating) required to optimize the energy from combustion expansion. In aviation engines, fuel use is limited to AVGAS 100 LL; later, we will discuss the specifics of this low-lead aviation fuel.

Additionally, the ratio between air mass and fuel that generates the explosion must be considered. This ratio is known as the "mixture ratio." We will delve into this concept later. For now, it's important to note that the mixture is a specific ratio of air and fuel that results in a controlled energy release explosion. In chemistry, this air-fuel ratio is referred to as the stoichiometric ratio, which defines the conditions where each constituent element is present in a specific amount to achieve the desired reaction—in this case, a controlled exothermic reaction of temperature and pressure.

Brayton Cycle

In contrast to the principles discussed in the preceding paragraphs, we will outline the generalities of the thermodynamic principle used by the jet engines mentioned earlier in this work.

The Brayton Cycle, also known as the Joule Cycle or Froude Cycle, is the thermodynamic principle of a compressible fluid (air), consisting of a compression stage, a heating stage, and an adiabatic expansion stage. This simple principle forms the basis for the operation of a multitude of processes in the industry, and above all, it is the fundamental theoretical basis of the jet engine.

The application of the gas turbine based on the Brayton Cycle to aerial propulsion is credited to the English engineer Frank Whittle, who patented the idea in 1927 and proposed it to the British Air Force. A series of experts led by Alan Arnold Griffith had studied in previous years the technical possibilities of the gas turbine as a means of aerial propulsion, although their idea was to use the mechanical work obtained to drive a propeller. Whittle, on the other hand, proposed a Brayton Cycle in which no net mechanical work was produced, so that the turbine would generate only enough energy to drive the compressor. According to him, propulsion would occur due to the high velocity of the gases exiting the turbine, creating a jet thrust force that would propel the engine.

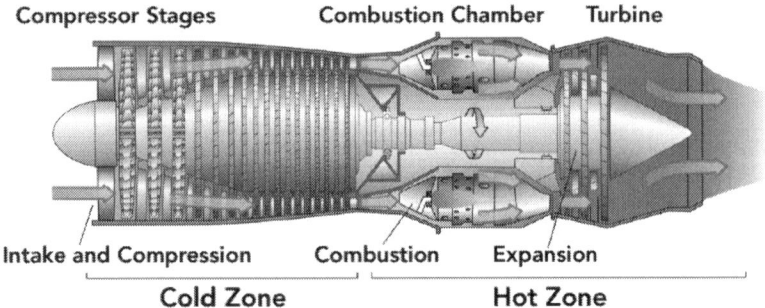

Compressor Stages   Combustion Chamber   Turbine

Intake and Compression   Combustion   Expansion

Cold Zone   **Hot Zone**

In this image, you can see the schematic of a turbojet engine (such as the Pratt Whitney JT3) without bypass flow. The arrows indicate the mass of air entering and undergoing compression in different stages. When the compressed mass reaches the combustion chambers, it mixes with fuel and undergoes combustion, characterized not by explosion but by a high release of pressure and temperature. The energy released drives the turbine stages and expands through the engine's exhaust nozzle, generating thrust force.

The non-explosive combustion is due to the use of high-performance fuels with high octane (or detonation) ratings. In the current aviation industry, the use of JET A-1 is standardized for such engines. JET A-1 is a refined kerosene byproduct with high energy-generating capacity and anti-detonation additives.

In this type of engine, the aircraft's propulsion capability is expressed in terms of thrust in kilograms-force (kgf), rather than horsepower (hp).

Atmospheric Variables

As previously mentioned, one crucial aspect in power generation is air. Air is essentially a portion of the entire atmospheric mass surrounding us. Therefore, it's important to recall some specifics that can modify or affect engine operation.

The atmosphere is composed of a combination of gases, primarily nitrogen with nearly one-third being oxygen. It's important to note that oxygen is the component of air mass involved in combustion. Below is a reminder of how atmospheric mass is composed at sea level.

The values depicted in the following graph are indicative and depend on numerous variables. Among the most important factors to consider are altitude and the time of year (such as wet, cold, or warm seasons).

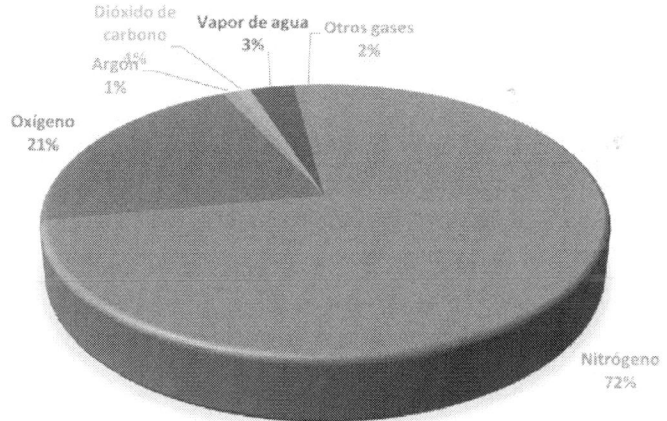

For instance, air in winter doesn't always contain more water vapor than in summer, yet it often feels more humid. This is because the vapor doesn't remain invisible gas but condenses into tiny droplets noticeable as wetness on the ground and exposed objects. Air can only hold a limited amount of water vapor relative to its temperature. When air holds all the water vapor it can at a given temperature, it's saturated, or at 100% humidity.

When the air's water vapor content is below saturation, it's described as having relative humidity (less than 100%). This is the ratio between the maximum grams of water vapor the air can hold and what it actually contains. The following table shows the relationship between temperature and the amount of water vapor air can hold, a critical factor for understanding subsequent content in the book.

Therefore, dew or frost isn't caused by water descending from heights like rain or snow but by the air's water vapor freezing.

TEMP °C	WATER VAPOR
-10	2,36
0	4,82
4	6,32
8	8,22
12	10,61
16	13,56
20	17,22
24	21,27
28	27,08
30	30,20

When the atmosphere reaches its maximum humidity, it can no longer hold more water vapor. Any additional vapor will condense into droplets or ice crystals. Saturation of air in the atmosphere is the precursor to cloud formation and can occur through various mechanisms such as local cooling in lower layers or the ascent of a humid air mass (which can be triggered by fronts, orographic relief, convection, etc.). Flying in clouds means being in a saturated air mass, prone to condensation into droplets and potentially freezing under certain conditions.

Introduction to Jet Engines

Understanding the basics of each system in the aircraft being piloted is among a pilot's responsibilities. This may seem overwhelming for trainee pilots at times, but it's crucial for pilots to identify, understand, and rectify faults and issues that may arise in emergency situations. Therefore, system training predominantly emphasizes understanding the operational sequence of each system, with particular focus on what happens if multiple components fail.

The systems of most modern turbine aircraft operate on similar principles but vary significantly in implementation details. Consequently, once you've learned the systems of one turbine aircraft, understanding others becomes much easier. Let's delve into the fundamental concepts of the main turbine aircraft systems.

The basic principle of operation of a gas turbine engine is straightforward. Jet propulsion is described by Isaac Newton's third law, which states that for every action, there is an equal and opposite reaction. In the broadest sense, gas turbine engines share jet propulsion with party balloons that have been inflated and released. In both cases, high-pressure gases escaping from a nozzle at one end create an equal and opposite force to propel each of these "reaction engines" in the opposite direction.

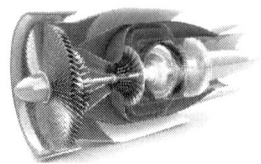

The main difference between a balloon and a gas turbine engine lies in the source of the propelling gases. A balloon is an energy storage device; someone blows air into it, and once the stored air escapes, the propulsion ends. Gas turbine engines, on the other hand, are heat engines. Through the combustion of fuel with intake air, they continuously create expanding gases, whose energy is converted into propulsive force to move an aircraft. For this reason, the core of a gas turbine engine is known as the gas generator; it generates the expanding gases needed to produce thrust. A nozzle is then used to accelerate the speed of the high-energy gases escaping from the gas generator. By increasing the pressure of the gases through its convergent-divergent chamber, a nozzle forces the gases out through its smaller exhaust opening. The effect of this process is an increase in the thrust of the air passing through the engine, producing propulsion.

The gas turbine engine can be compared in basic operational stages to its distant relative, the internal combustion engine (also known as a "piston engine" or "reciprocating engine"). As you may recall, most aircraft piston engines operate in a sequence of four strokes: intake, compression, power (or combustion), and exhaust. The power developed by a piston engine is intermittent, as only one out of every four strokes (the power stroke) actually creates power. Parallel stages occur in gas turbine engines, but with a fundamental difference: gas turbines operate under more efficient continuous flow conditions.

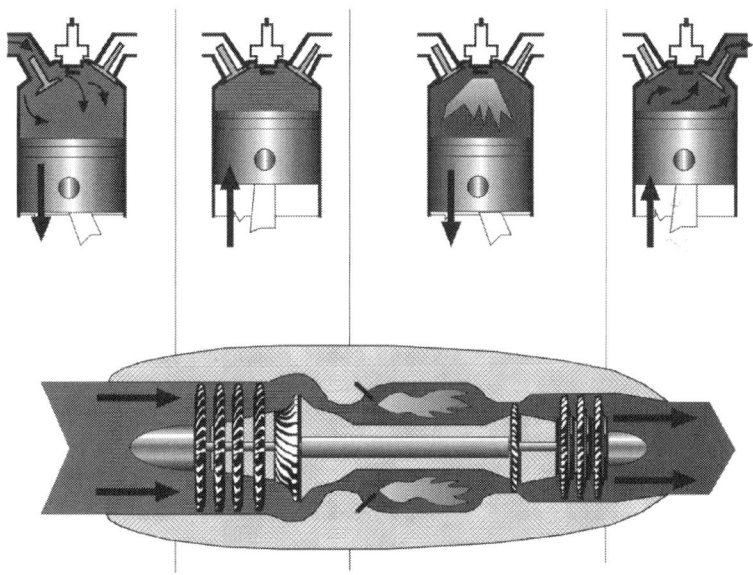

Instead of compressing the intake air with a piston, turbine engines use one or more "wheels" with rotating blades in the compressor section known as compressors. Another set of wheels is driven by the exhaust gases passing through the turbine section.

Instead of compressing the intake air with a piston, turbine engines use one or more "wheels" with rotating blades in the compressor section known as compressors. Another set of wheels is driven by the exhaust gases passing through the turbine section.

Instead of compressing the intake air with a piston, turbine engines use one or more "wheels" with rotating blades in the compressor section known as compressors. Another set of wheels is driven by the exhaust gases passing through the turbine section.

Instead of compressing the intake air with a piston, turbine engines use one or more "wheels" with rotating blades in the compressor section known as compressors. Another set of wheels is driven by the exhaust gases passing through the turbine section.

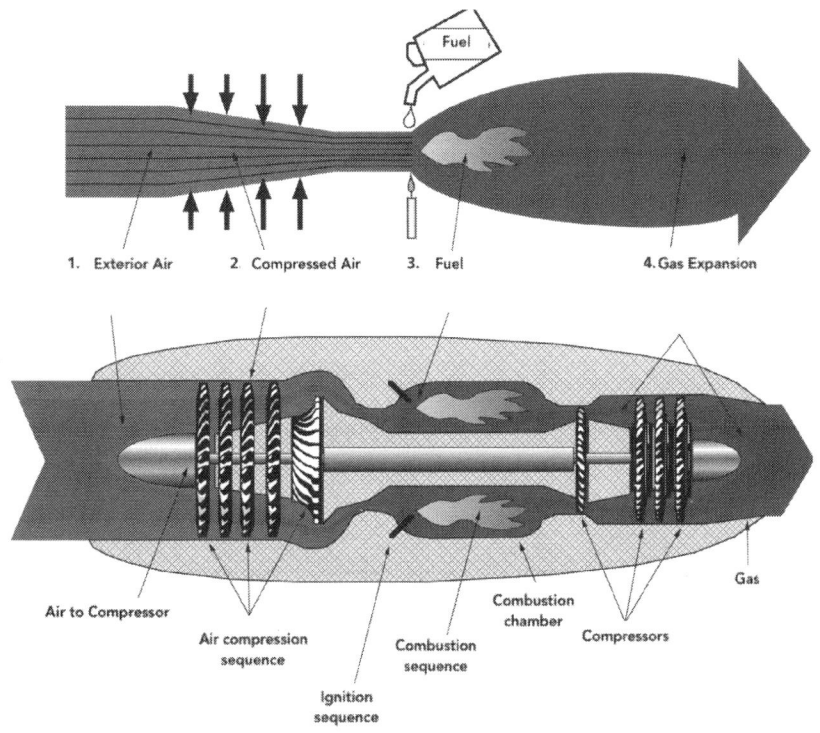

1. Exterior Air   2. Compressed Air   3. Fuel   4. Gas Expansion

Air to Compressor

Air compression
sequence

Ignition
sequence

Combustion
sequence

Combustion
chamber

Compressors

Gas

Centrifugal Flow Compressor

A centrifugal flow compressor uses an impeller similar to that of a turbocharger. The engine's air intake directs the incoming air towards the center of the impeller, where it is thrown outward in a centrifugal manner towards a carefully designed chamber known as a "diffuser." A diffuser is simply a diverging duct that slows down the exit velocity of the air from the impeller, thereby increasing the air pressure before it enters the combustion chamber.

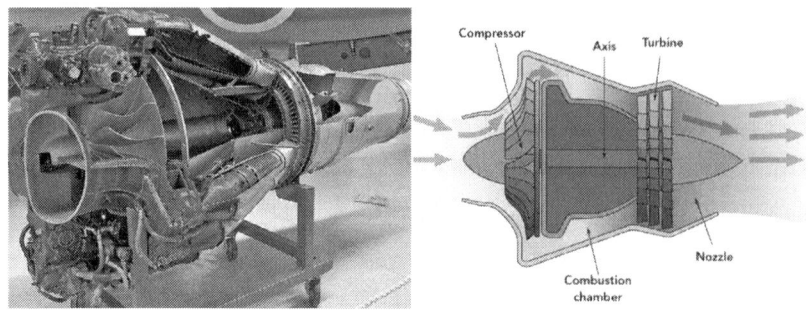

The airflow through an axial flow compressor, on the other hand, remains essentially parallel to the engine's longitudinal axis; the air is not thrown outward in the diffuser as with the centrifugal flow compressor. An axial flow compressor is composed of a alternating series of rotating rotor blades and stationary stator blades. Inlet air enters the first set of rotor blades, where it is redirected in the direction of rotation. The stationary stator blades between each set of rotor blades help direct and compress the airflow. The goal is to maintain the airflow essentially parallel to the engine's longitudinal axis between each set of rotor blades. In this sense, an axial flow compressor functions more like a window fan, whereas a centrifugal flow compressor throws the air outward like a slingshot.

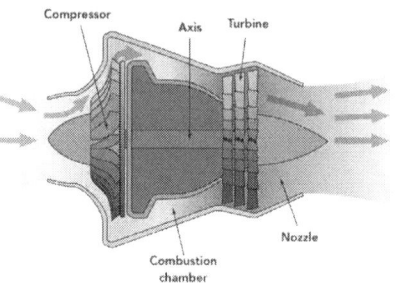

Centrifugal flow compressors are more durable than axial flow models. Turboprop aircraft and many corporate jets use centrifugal flow compressors because these aircraft are more likely to operate from unprepared airstrips than large aircraft. On the other hand, axial flow compressors are more efficient. While a centrifugal flow compressor typically achieves a compression ratio of 10:1, an axial flow model can achieve ratios of over 25:1. This means engines with axial flow compressors can produce more thrust for the same frontal area, resulting in less aerodynamic drag and greater fuel efficiency. Large jets use axial flow compressors due to the higher compression ratio, which provides greater thrust-to-weight ratio and fuel efficiency

Multistage compressor

In order to maximize efficiency and power, most modern turbine engines use more than one compressor component, each aligned sequentially behind the other. A combination of axial flow and centrifugal compressors can be used, or there may be multiple components of the same type. In both cases, each compressor "wheel" or row of rotor blades and stator blades acts as a compressor stage. Each compressor stage progressively compresses the gases passing through one step beyond the previous stage.

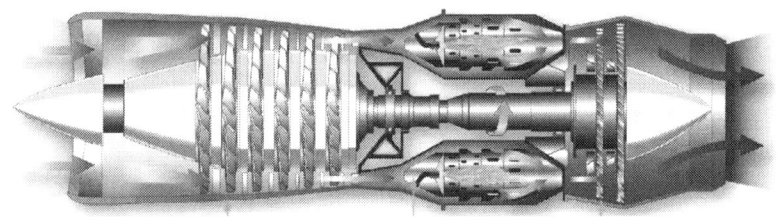

The compressor components can be mounted on the same shaft or on different nested shafts. A set of multiple compressor stages is known as a multi-stage compressor, with the number of stages corresponding to the number of compressor components.

To clarify this terminology, it's important to note that each axial flow compressor is inherently multi-stage. As discussed earlier, an axial flow compressor consists of several rotating "wheels" with blades between them. Each row of rotor blades with their stator blades forms a compressor stage. However, the entire assembly is considered a single compressor as long as all rotating parts are mounted on a common shaft.

Multiple compressor engines

Many gas turbine engines feature two tandem compressors mounted on separate shafts that rotate at different speeds. These dual-compressor engines offer higher compression ratios compared to single-compressor models.

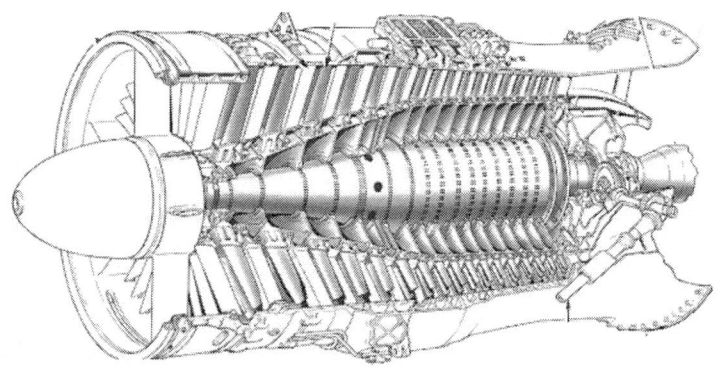

Single compressor engine

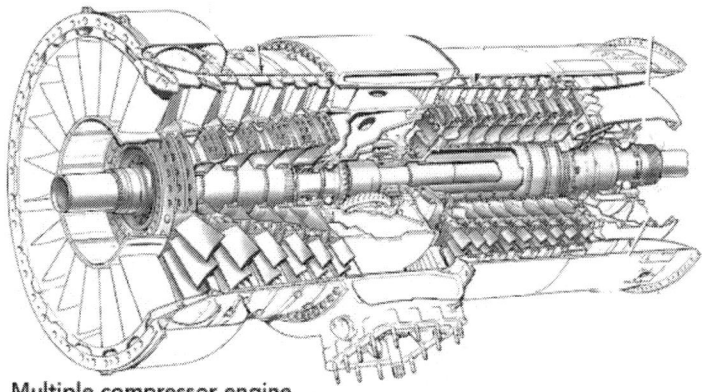

Multiple compressor engine

The forward-most compressor in a dual-compressor engine is known as the low-pressure compressor. It is driven by the low-pressure turbine shaft, located at the rear of the engine. Both are interconnected through the low-pressure compressor shaft. The rotational speed of a low-pressure compressor is referred to as "N1"; thus, the low-pressure compressor shaft is commonly known as the N1 shaft.

The second compressor in a dual-compressor engine is called the high-pressure compressor. It is powered by its own high-pressure turbine through a high-pressure hollow shaft (or N2 shaft), which rotates concentrically around the N1 shaft. As you may have deduced, N2 represents the speed of the high-pressure compressor.

To clarify the terminology further, let's describe a dual axial compressor. This incorporates a nine-stage axial low-pressure compressor on one shaft, followed by a seven-stage axial high-pressure compressor on a separate shaft. Both rotate independently at different speeds.

Each compressor, its driving turbine, and the connecting shaft are collectively known as a "spool." By examining the two separate spools of a dual-compressor engine, one can appreciate the distinctive shape of each spool.

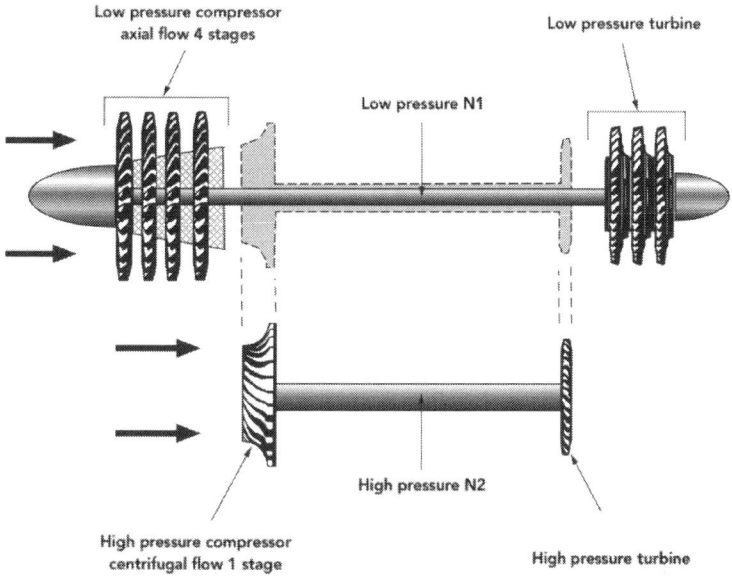

Low-Pressure Spool

Low pressure compressor
axial flow 4 stages

Low pressure turbine

Low pressure N1

High pressure N2

High pressure compressor
centrifugal flow 1 stage

High pressure turbine

High-Pressure Spool

Main gas turbine engine

Turbine engines exist in many variants. Models can be found with one, two, or three spools, using any combination of centrifugal and axial flow compressors. Additionally, any number of compressor and turbine stages can be incorporated into each spool. These engine design details vary significantly depending on the type of engine and the manufacturer. While these differences impact the performance and reliability of competing turbine engines, their basic layout and functions remain the same. Each gas turbine engine is built around

31

the same core components, which include compressor sections, combustion chamber, and turbines.

The basic gas turbine engine we have been discussing is commonly known as a gas generator or main turbine engine. To familiarize with the terminology in English, we will show some descriptive images with the different sections in English.

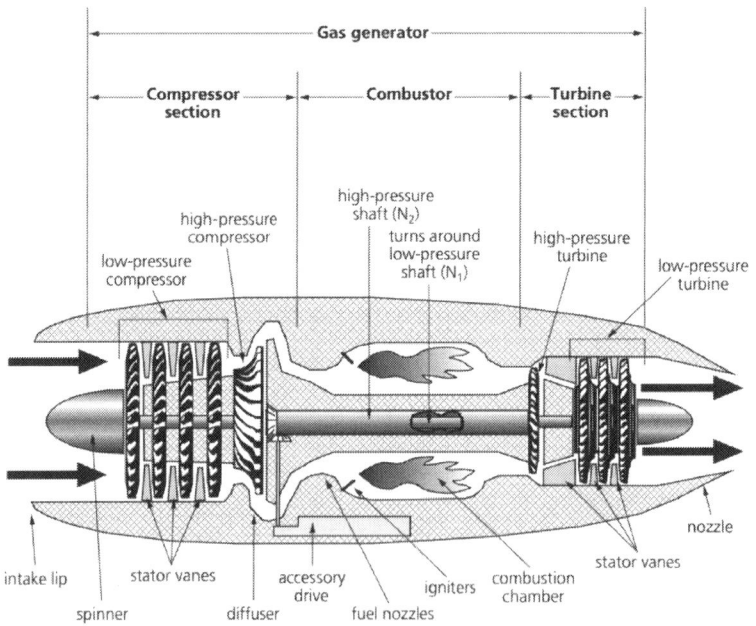

Our "typical" gas generator has a four-stage axial flow low-pressure compressor, followed by a single-stage centrifugal high-pressure compressor. Its turbine section incorporates a single-stage high-pressure turbine and a three-stage low-pressure turbine. (This arrangement is just an example and does not aim to represent any specific engine).

32

Turborreactors, Turbofans, and Turboprops

Despite the various variations of turbine engines, the basic operating principles of the main turbine engine remain the same. Depending on how exhaust gases are utilized, the same basic gas generator can be applied to turbojet engines, turbofans, or turboprops. The largest conceptual difference between these engines lies in how engine power is translated into thrust to propel an aircraft.

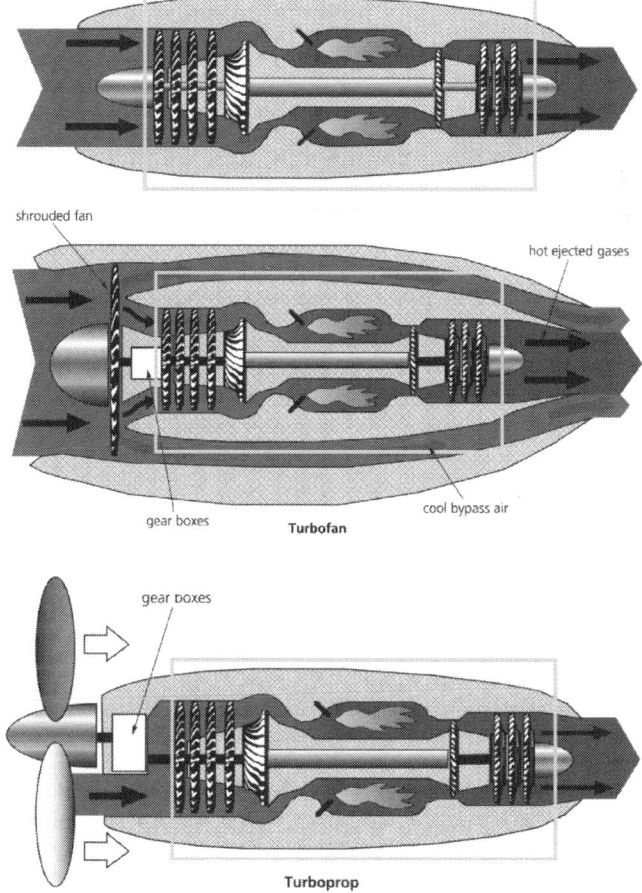

Turborreactors

The gas turbine engines discussed so far are known as turbojet engines. A turbojet engine generates thrust solely through high acceleration of air passing through and expelled by the main engine. The earliest jet engines were of this type. Turbojet engines, while performing well at high altitudes and high airspeeds, are highly inefficient at low altitudes and low airspeeds. They are also noisier and less fuel-efficient compared to modern turbofan engines.

Turbofan

A turbofan engine utilizes the same basic core engine as a turbojet. The difference lies in a "ducted fan" located at the front of the engine, driven by the engine's turbine section. (A ducted fan is essentially a propeller with multiple blades enclosed within a close-fitting casing). A turbofan accelerates a larger mass of air than a turbojet. Some of the intake air bypasses the main engine core, flowing around the exterior. This bypass air generates significant thrust due to the highly efficient design of the turbofan blades.

The ratio of bypass air flowing through the engine's fan section compared to the amount of air flowing through the gas generator part of the engine is called the engine's bypass ratio. For most corporate and airline aircraft designs, engines with higher bypass ratios are more fuel-efficient. (To give an idea of the quantities involved, airflow through the engine is measured in pounds per second).

Turbofan engines with small amounts of bypass thrust are called low-bypass engines or simply bypass engines. Engines with large amounts of fan bypass thrust are known as high-bypass turbofan engines. At lower altitudes, more than 80 percent of the thrust from a high-bypass engine comes from the ducted fan, resulting in greater fuel efficiency.

Turbofans emerged because "ducted fans" (in this case, the enclosed turbofan blades) are more efficient than jet thrust at relatively low altitudes and airspeeds. Essentially, a turbofan engine represents a compromise between the best features of turbojets and turboprops, with turbojets being most suitable for high altitudes and high airspeeds, and turboprops being most efficient at low altitudes and relatively low airspeeds.

Turbojets are very noisy due to the high-speed exhaust gases colliding with surrounding cool air, creating a deafening wind shear noise. However, turbofans are much quieter because of the mixing of cool bypass air with the hot exhaust gases from the main engine. This helps to isolate and disperse the hot exhaust gases, significantly dampening the noise. Virtually all jet engines in production today are turbofans.

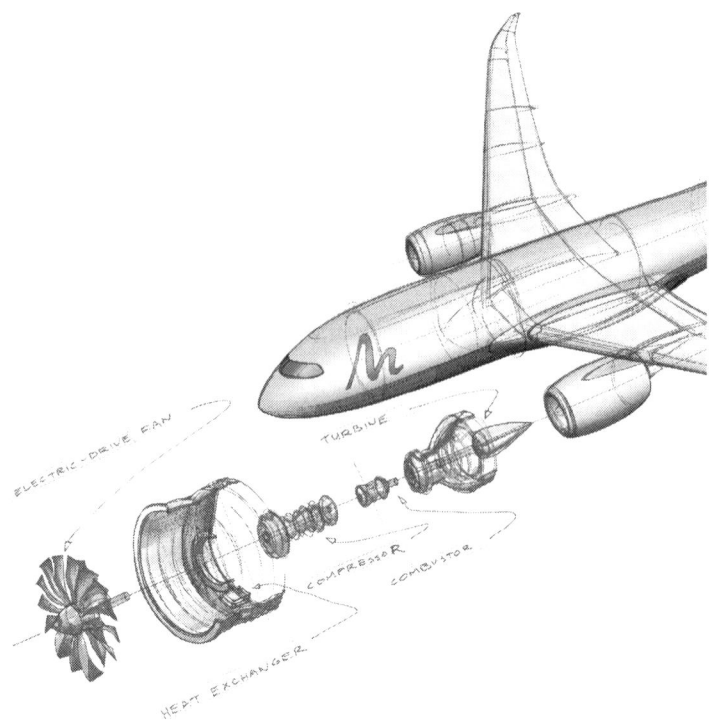

Turboprop

UA turboprop engine simply utilizes the thrust generated by a main turbine engine to drive a propeller. The turbine of a turboprop engine is designed to absorb significant amounts of energy and deliver it in the form of torque to the propeller. There are two different ways of achieving this. In a direct drive turboprop engine, the propeller is driven directly from the compressor shaft through a set of reduction gears.

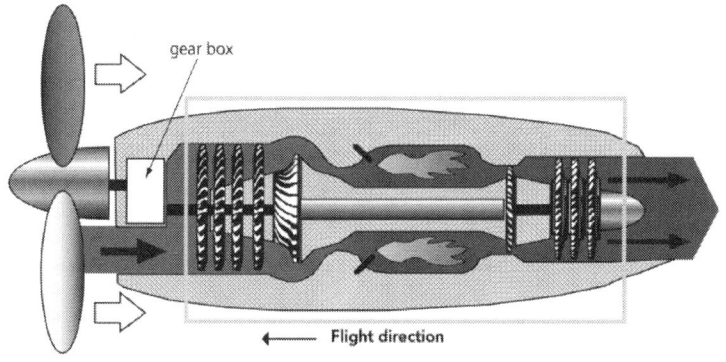

gear box

Flight direction

In a free turbine turboprop engine, the propeller is not directly connected to the core of the engine. Instead, an additional "power section" of free turbine is added to the basic engine core after the turbine section. High-pressure exhaust gases from the core engine are used to drive the free power turbine. The power turbine, in turn, spins a shaft that moves the propeller gearbox. This non-mechanical connection between the engine core and the propeller transmission shaft is known as a fluid coupling. The same principle is used in automatic transmissions of cars, except in turboprop engines it is gaseous rather than liquid.

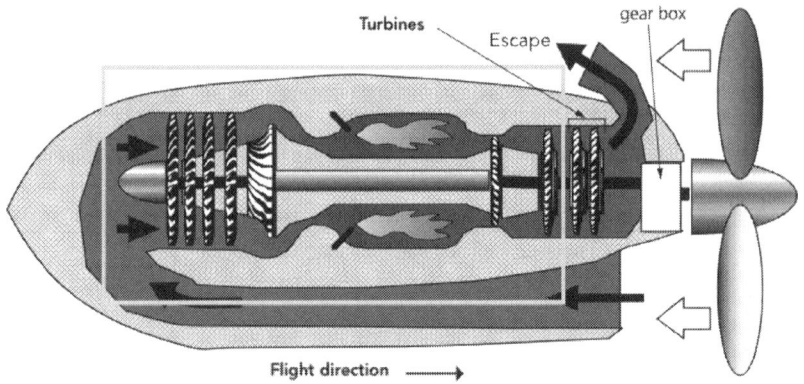

Turbines, Escape, gear box, Flight direction

The design difference between direct drive and free turbine engines can easily be identified after engine shutdown. When a pilot manually rotates the propeller of a direct drive turboprop, they are also turning the engine core, meaning the engine is relatively difficult to turn. But with a free turbine turboprop, the only turbine spinning with the propeller is the power turbine driving it, allowing these engines' propellers to often rotate freely in the wind. Since there is no mechanical connection between the propeller and the engine core in this case, the engine core does not rotate when the propeller is turned by hand.

Both direct drive and free turbine engines have distinct advantages and disadvantages. Direct drive engines are designed to operate at more or less fixed RPMs. Adding power (by adding fuel) results in increased power without significant change in RPM. This means that the internal aerodynamics of the compressor section, combustion chamber, and turbine section can be finely tuned to the optimal operating range.

For this reason, direct drive turboprop engines offer more immediate power response and are more fuel-efficient. Idle speed on the ground for direct drive engines is high (around 72 percent of maximum RPM), as the propeller is directly connected to the engine core. Therefore, this type of engine generates significant noise on the ground (Propellers are responsible for most of the "engine noise" in any propeller-driven aircraft).

A free turbine turboprop, on the other hand, has relatively low noise levels at idle on the ground. The RPM speed of the engine core is lower in this type, and since there is no mechanical connection between the engine core and the propeller, the propeller can slow down even more slowly.

Another significant advantage of some free turbine engines is that they can be easily disassembled for servicing, often without needing to be removed from the aircraft. The popular Pratt & Whitney PT-6 series of free turbine engines optimizes this principle through its "reverse flow" installation.

Air is directed toward the rear of the engine to enter the rear-mounted compressor section, allowing the power section to be directly mounted on the propeller gearbox. Since the power section (including the free power turbine) is not physically connected to the gas generator except through the engine casing and pipes, either section can be relatively easily removed from the aircraft for maintenance.

However, the internal aerodynamics of a free turbine turboprop must be designed to operate over a wider range of pressures and airspeeds. Therefore, a free turbine engine tends to operate with less optimal internal aerodynamics than its direct drive counterparts. This makes the free turbine turboprop less powerful in relation to its weight and less fuel-efficient than the direct drive type.

It is easy to distinguish whether a turboprop aircraft is of the direct drive or free turbine type. Observe the angle of the propeller blades after shutdown. If the propellers are at a very low blade angle relative to their plane of rotation (i.e., in fine pitch), the turboprop is of the direct drive type. If the propellers are in the "feathered" position, the turboprop is of the free turbine type.

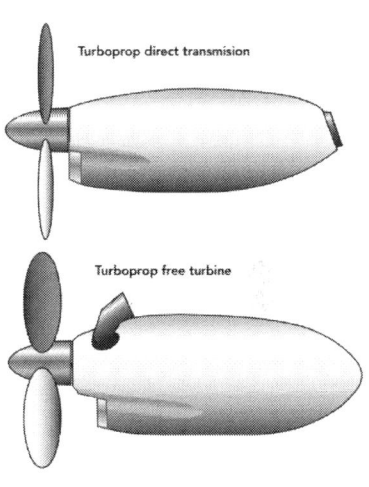

This difference occurs because direct drive turboprops have start locks that fix the propeller blades at a 0° blade angle after shutdown. Start locks are metal pins held by centrifugal force at operating RPM, allowing the blade angle to change. But when RPM drops below a certain level upon shutdown, start locks move inward towards the propeller hub and lock the propeller at a low blade angle. Upon starting the engine, the propellers must rotate along with the engine due to their rigid connection, and the flat pitch position reduces air resistance during startup. If the blades were in the "feathered" position, it would be more difficult to rotate the propeller at startup.

Free turbine turboprops do not need start locks because there is no direct connection between the propeller and the engine core. The engine, therefore, can be easily started as the mass and resistance of the propeller do not restrict the RPM of the engine core. The propeller starts to rotate only when the engine core produces enough exhaust gases to spin the power turbine. Therefore, propellers on free turbine turboprops may move to their "feathered" position naturally upon shutdown.

Thrust or power?

The output of turbine engines was referred to as "thrust" until we reached turboprops. Then, the discussion shifted to "power". This is because the definition of "power," commonly used for piston engines, does

not translate well to pure turbine engines. Power is defined as force applied over a distance per unit of time. However, jet engines generate thrust in the air without moving any mechanical parts over a distance. Consequently, jet engines are classified in pounds of thrust.

However, turboprops do generate power in the form of torque, which is force applied to a propeller over a distance of rotation. Therefore, turboprops are classified using power-related terminology. Shaft power refers to the power delivered by a turboprop engine to its propeller. However, the exhaust gases from the core of turboprops also produce a certain jet thrust that increases the propeller's output. The effect of jet thrust adds to the shaft power rating of the turboprop to produce a total power rating known as equivalent shaft power. Note this difference when discussing engine management in turbine aircraft. Turboprop pilots adjust power or torque. Jet pilots adjust thrust.

Engine parameters

The output of a turbine engine can be measured and expressed in various ways. In jet engines, Engine Pressure Ratio (EPR) refers to the ratio between the engine outlet pressure and the engine inlet pressure. Therefore, the higher the EPR, the greater the thrust being produced. (When the inlet pressure and outlet pressure of the engine are equal, i.e., when EPR = 1, the engine is not producing thrust.)

While EPR is commonly used to adjust thrust in turbojet and turbofan engines, the power of turboprops is commonly adjusted and monitored in pounds-feet of torque (or sometimes as a percentage of maximum torque) delivered to the propeller transmission system.

Other common parameters for turbine engine operation are expressed in terms of RPM (revolutions per minute) of the different shafts within the engine. As you recall, N1 typically refers to the RPM of the low-pressure compressor shaft, while N2 refers to the RPM of the high-pressure power shaft. N1 and N2 are often expressed as percentages of a value close to maximum RPM, as they represent very high numbers.

However, maximum RPM is not always 100 percent. In some business jet turbofans, N1 is the primary instrument for adjusting thrust, rather than EPR.

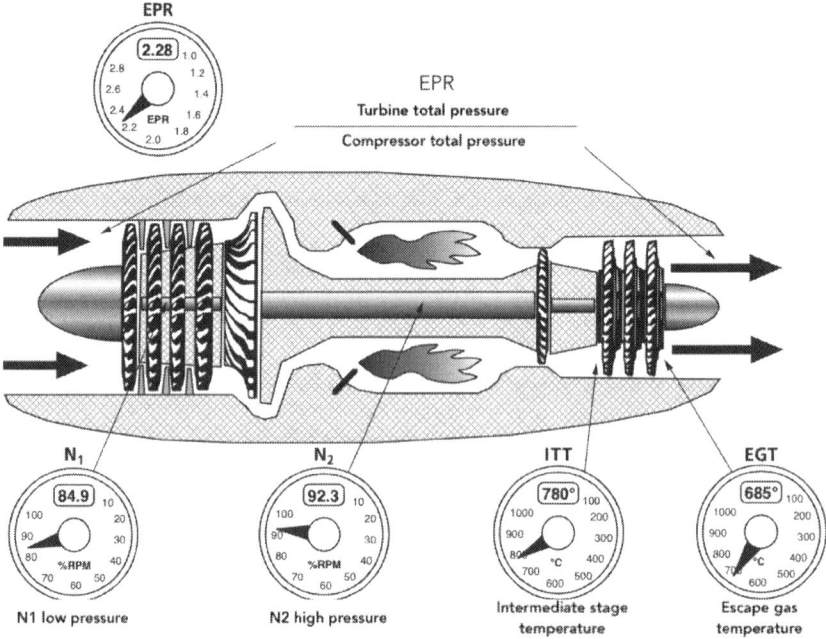

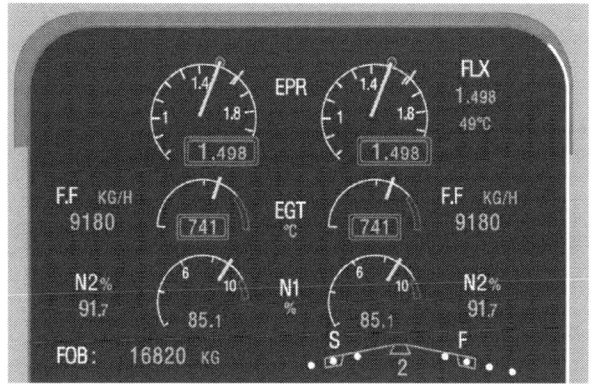

Similar to piston engines, temperature control is crucial in turbine powerplant. Depending on the type and installation of the engine, Exhaust Gas Temperature (EGT) or Interstage Turbine Temperature (ITT) are commonly used for this purpose. Fuel flow indicators also provide useful control parameters in turbine engines.

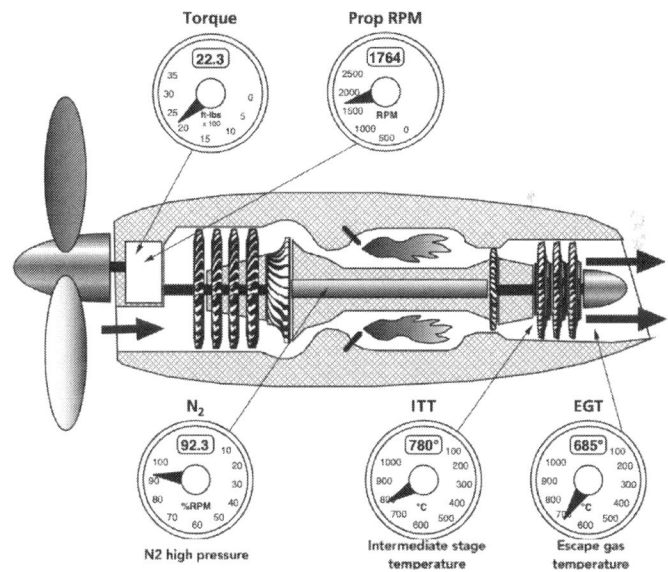

45

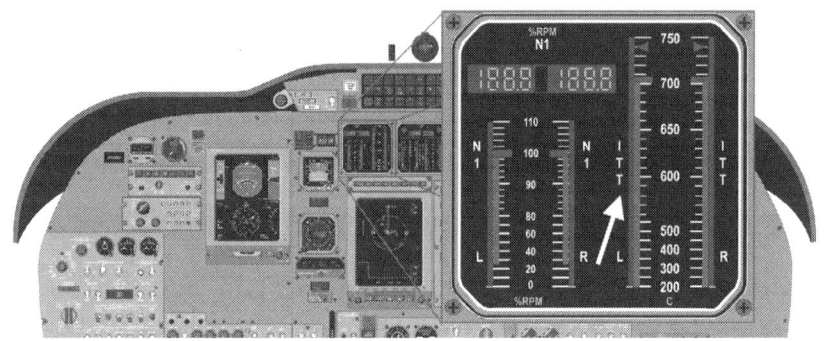

The engine control system

Managing thrust or power is straightforward for turbine engines. Typically, primary engine controls in jets consist simply of thrust levers. Separate start levers are sometimes used to start and stop fuel flow to the engines.

In turboprop engines, power levers or torque levers replace throttles, while fuel levers on turboprops are commonly referred to as condition levers. Most turboprops are equipped with a separate propeller RPM control (similar to those found in piston engines), although in some cases, propeller control is integrated into the power levers (e.g., Saab 2000) or condition levers (e.g., Dash-8).

Jet engine start

A jet engine operates marvelously once running, unlikely to stop unless fuel or air supply is interrupted, or there's a mechanical failure. However, starting it is a bit more complex.

At some point, you may have wondered what ensures that the expanding gases exit the engine's correct end. This isn't a silly question. Enough air must be compressed in the combustion chamber(s) so that when fuel is added and ignited, the energized combustion gases travel rearward through the turbine section instead of forward.

Imagine the compressed air wall entering the combustion chamber like an invisible cylinder head, and the turbine section like a piston in a reciprocating engine. It's crucial during the starting sequence of a jet engine to spin the compressor section fast enough to build the air wall at the front of the combustion chamber. This ensures that the flow of combustion gases travels backward once the fuel-air mixture ignites and that compression is sufficiently high for a good start.

When these conditions aren't met, there's a risk of a hot start. A hot start occurs when fuel is introduced while the compressor rotation speed is too low, resulting in inadequate pressures in the combustion chamber. In this situation, the fuel burns at very high temperatures in the combustion chamber with little or no flow to the turbine section. If the pilot doesn't recognize this situation immediately through careful monitoring, the engine can overheat and be ruined within seconds.

In smaller turbine engines, the compressor is typically spun for starting by an electric starter motor. For larger turbine engines, high-pressure air drives a pneumatic starter motor. This high-pressure air can come from various sources such as an auxiliary power unit (APU), ground air supply, or cross-bleed air from another engine.

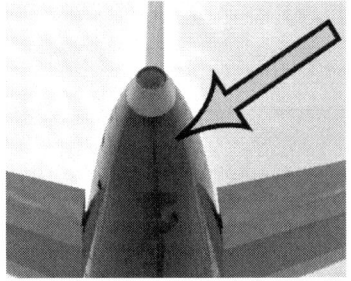

Turbine engines use igniters to ignite the fuel-air mixture during starting. Some igniters are glow plugs, similar to those used in diesel engines (they include a resistance coil through which electric current flows to heat them until they glow steadily). Others are similar to spark plugs found in piston engines, emitting a steady stream of sparks to ignite the mixture.

Once the engine's fuel-air mixture ignites, the igniters can be turned off. Similar to a welding torch, combustion in a turbine engine is sustained simply by continuously injecting fuel into the burning gases of the combustion chamber. The regulator can directly or indirectly control the amount of fuel (depending on the engine manufacturer). The energized combustion gases then travel rearward to drive the power turbines, as discussed earlier.

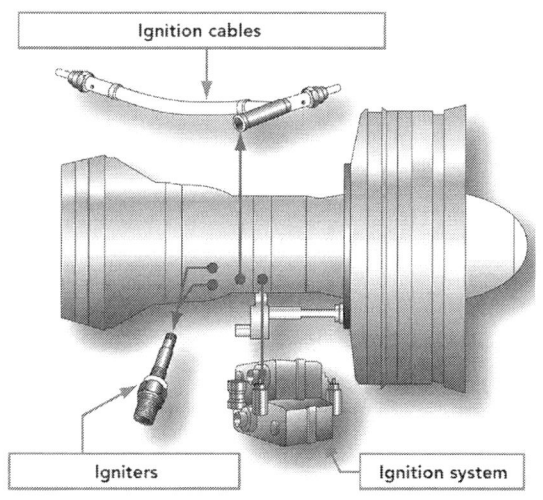

Engine start procedure Airbus A320

As an example, let's analyze the engine start procedure on one of the world's most flown aircraft, the Airbus A320 model.

In this image, the monitoring screen is observed to be off, indicating that the aircraft has not yet been powered up.

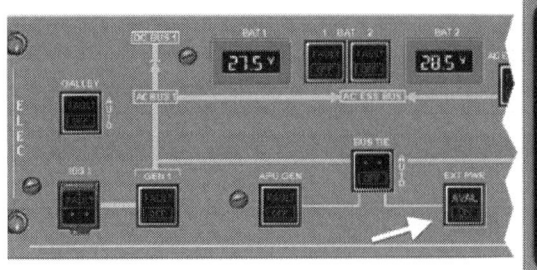

To power up the aircraft, the pilot activates the ground power unit (GPU) external power system, and the aircraft begins to power up and turn on its displays:

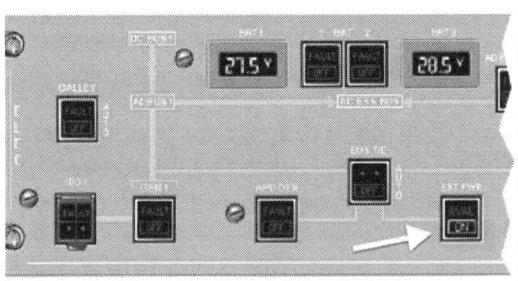

One of the primary tasks for starting the engine is supplying the system with bleed air to enable ignition. With the APU system, it is possible to supply air to the engines through the APU BLEED subsystem. Once this preliminary action is completed, the pilot can proceed with the automatic engine start.

The first step for engine start is to turn the ENG MODE SELECTOR knob from the NORMAL position to the IGN/START position.

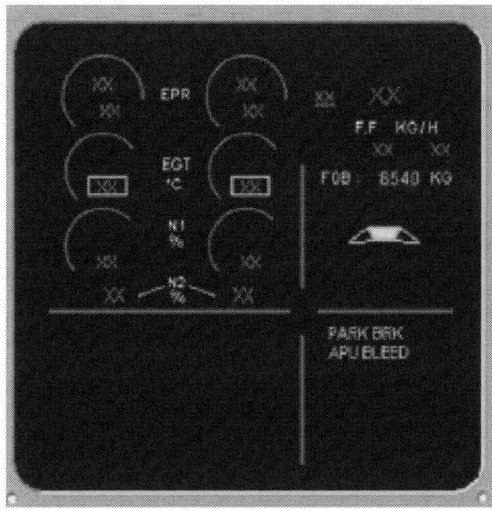

Before turning the knob, the engine parameters on the E/WD display all show crosses with no information. When the pilot switches the knob to the IGN/START position, the system activates and information begins to appear.

On the ECAM Warning Display, the crosses disappear and engine parameters start to display, currently all off but visible. Additionally, selecting IGN/START mode also activates other engine parameters on the ENGINE page of the ECAM System Display.

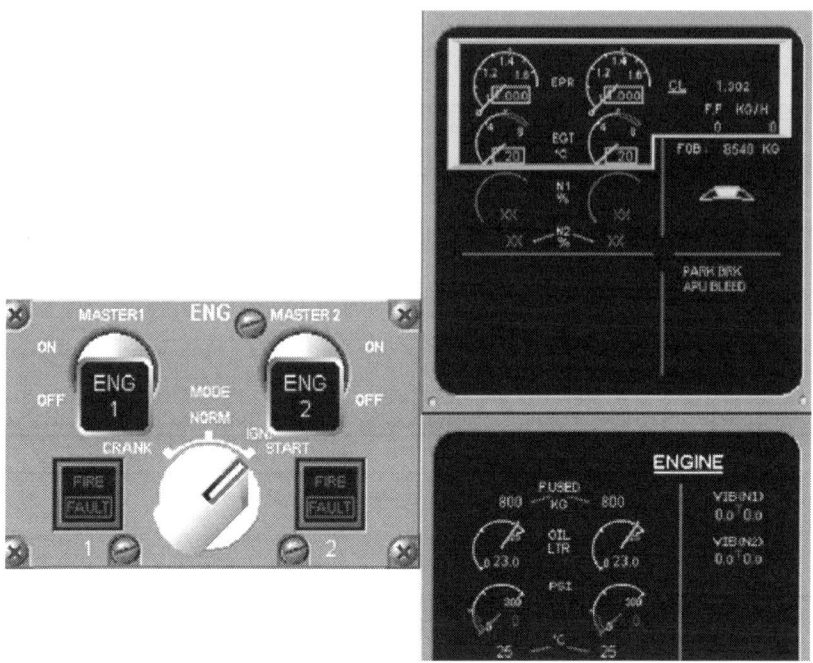

The next step will be to activate the master switch for each engine, but before proceeding, let's review the information provided by the two ECAM displays about the engines and their various variables.

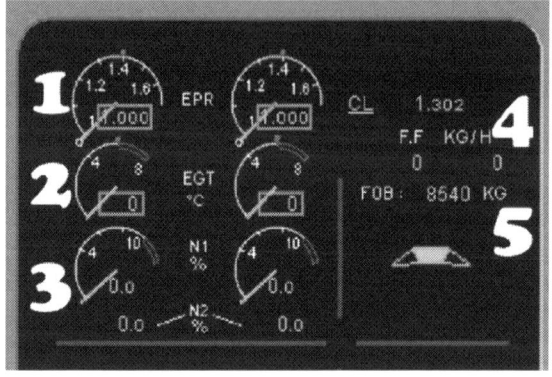

Starting with the E/WD, point one indicates the Engine Pressure Ratio (EPR) for both engines. Point two displays the Exhaust Gas Temperature (EGT) for both engines. Point three shows the values of N1 and N2, and finally, points four and five represent fuel values: FF (Fuel Flow) for each engine and FOB (Fuel on Board) Total. Just below the E/WD, the ECAM system display activates and shows the ENGINE page with the following information:

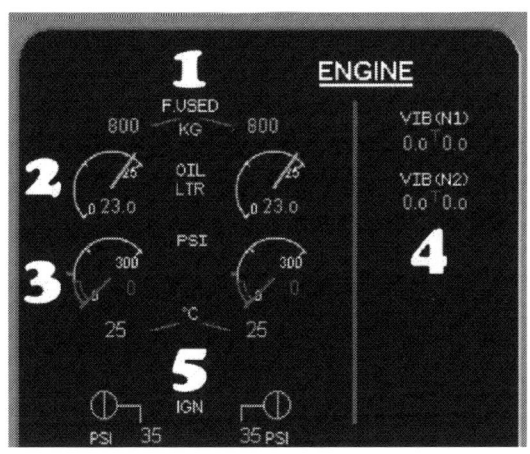

Starting with the E/WD, point one indicates the Engine Pressure Ratio (EPR) for both engines. Point two displays the Exhaust Gas Temperature (EGT) for both engines. Point three shows the values of N1 and N2, and finally, points four and five represent fuel values: FF (Fuel Flow) for each engine and FOB (Fuel on Board) Total. Just below the E/WD, the ECAM system display activates and shows the ENGINE page with the following information:

The system is ready to start an engine. Let's begin with engine number two. Simply change the MASTER SWITCH from OFF to ON by lifting the knob.

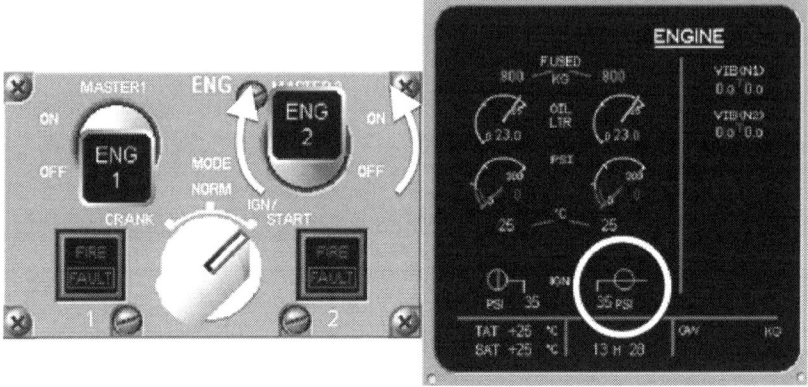

The first indication that changes its information is the START VALVE in the ignition sector on the ECAM, moving from the closed to the open position. Upon completion of this process, other indications begin to appear. Let's see:

Typically, engine start procedures begin with engine number two, aiming to pressurize the yellow hydraulic system and release the use of the electric pump for system pressurization. After the START VALVE opens, the Fuel Used resets to zero, as shown in point one of the following image:

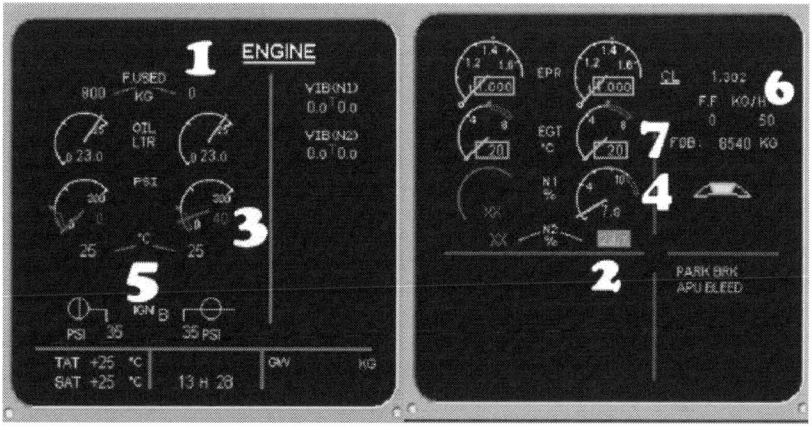

Following that, at point two, we observe the initial indication of N2 increasing. Returning to the ECAM Lower Display, at point three, the oil pressure begins to rise. Subsequently, at point four, we start seeing indications of N1 while ignition system B is activated (point five), initiating the start-up process. Upon successful completion of this process, at point six, we begin to observe the Fuel Flow indication, and finally, the EPR begins to rise at point seven.

When the N2 value reaches 43%, the START VALVE closes, signaling the completion of the start-up procedure. N2 continues to increase until stabilizing at approximately 58%, indicating the engine is fully operational and ready for use. The next step will be to initiate the same start-up procedure for engine number one, completing the start-up of both engines. We will consider this step completed as it is exactly identical to the previous one, but with observations of engine number one's indications.

As soon as both engines have their N2 values stabilized and fully started, in the lower right margin of the ECAM Lower Display, the GW (gross weight) or total weight of the aircraft information appears, as shown in the circle in the image.

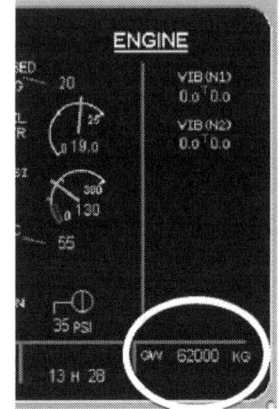

Finally, to complete the start-up, we only need to return the ENG MODE SELECTOR to the NORMAL position by turning the knob back to the left.

Chapter 2

Jet engine associated systems

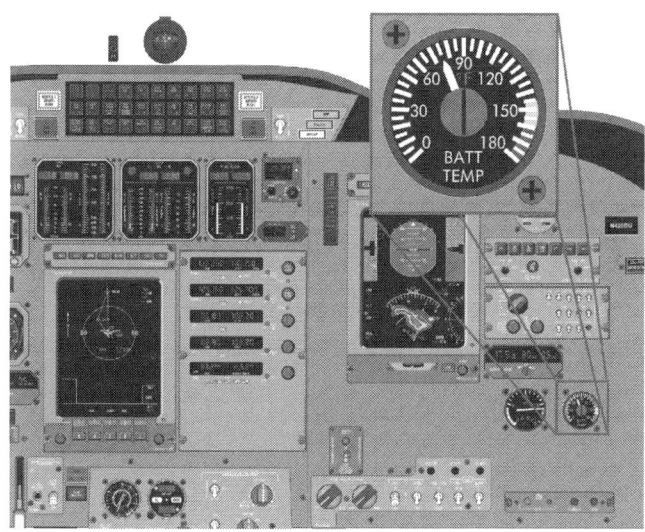

Introduction

In aircraft, engines not only provide the necessary power for propulsion but are also crucial for the operation of associated or secondary systems linked to each engine. In this chapter, we will explore how these systems function in relation to jet engines.

Associated systems

Nearly all the energy required to operate a turbine-powered aircraft ultimately comes from one source: engine power. (The small remaining amount comes from pilots physically operating controls.) After examining how engines work, let's now consider the systems that transfer engine power to where it's needed to operate the aircraft. For redundancy and functionality, there are essentially four ways to transmit power throughout the aircraft: mechanical, electrical, hydraulic, and pneumatic.

While each of these four power systems has unique advantages, some features and terms apply universally. The four systems are interconnected to provide various protections and functions. Often, one power system controls another in specific applications. For example, an electrical solenoid valve may be used to direct hydraulic power to the correct side of a landing gear hydraulic motor for retraction or extension. Other examples include

59

pneumatic valves that activate electrical switches, manual levers that move pneumatic valves, and electrically controlled hydraulic cylinders that operate landing gear doors. Any combination is possible.

One purpose of such arrangements is to influence what happens in case of different types of failures. If electrical power is lost, how will various valves and switches fail? What about a hydraulic failure? Critical switches and valves are designed to operate predictably in the event of specific system failures.

Electrical system

While electrical systems are fundamentally similar across all aircraft, turbine-powered airplanes have the complexity of numerous electrical systems. They operate under extreme temperatures, altitude, and humidity conditions, requiring extensive cabin environmental systems and passenger amenities. Consequently, the electrical systems of these aircraft are complex, sophisticated, and redundant to ensure safety. It's crucial to remember that a functioning electrical circuit must always form a complete loop. If the electrical circuit is interrupted, the system ceases to function.

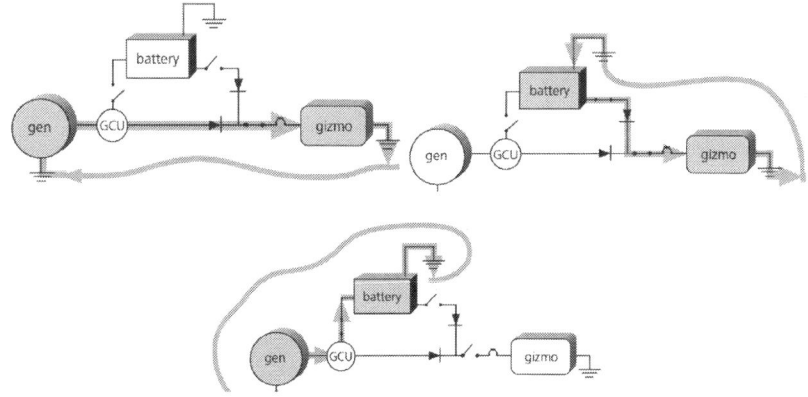

In aircraft, cables carry electrical power to devices in each circuit. The "return" of electricity to complete each circuit typically flows through the aircraft's metal structure, also known as ground. Each electrical system is composed of one or more circuits containing power sources, components powered by each circuit, control devices to operate the circuits, and circuit protection devices to safeguard system components from damage due to faults.

Electrical system sources

Generator

The engine-driven generator in the aircraft's electrical system serves as its core. The generator outputs are measured using parameters of pressure and flow volume. Electrically, the generator's output voltage is measured in volts (V), representing its electrical pressure. Its output volume or flow is known as current, measured in amperes (amps)

Generators generate electricity by moving permanent magnets around a coil of wire, inducing electron flow in the coil. In modern aircraft, generators are powered by the engine and sometimes by an Auxiliary Power Unit (APU), if installed. Similar to how a water pump pressurizes a sealed water system up to its own pressure, a generator drives its associated circuit practically to its own voltage. Since generators are designed to produce more or less constant voltage, the power required to drive various components is always defined in terms of current (amps). The current needed to operate each electrical component relative to the circuit is known as its load.

Therefore, a generator must have an adequate nominal amperage capacity to power all components operating within its circuit. For example, if a circuit has six devices, each with a nominal capacity of 5 amps, a generator dedicated to that circuit needs to supply at least 30 amps (5 amps × 6 devices) to operate all six devices simultaneously.

Of course, in an aircraft, each generator powers many circuits. Sometimes, generators may not be able to provide enough power for everything that is turned on. An example would be the failure of one of the engine-driven generators in a twin-engine aircraft. While two operational generators will power most things in the aircraft simultaneously, one alone might not suffice. In such a case, it would be necessary to perform an electrical load shedding. (No, throwing anything out the window is not necessary). Sufficient electrical equipment must be turned off to reduce the electrical load within the capacity of the operational generator. Some electrical systems are designed to automatically perform "load shedding."

Some words are necessary regarding generator terminology. In automobiles and light aircraft, the term "generator" has been associated with a device that generates direct current (DC), while alternators produce alternating current (AC). However, in turbine-powered aircraft, you will generally hear these devices referred to as "DC generators" and "AC generators."

Most modern aircraft are electrically powered by AC generators. Especially in large aircraft, most high-power electrical devices (such as electric hydraulic pumps and windshield heaters) operate on AC. AC is then converted to DC to power DC systems. Some aircraft have both AC and DC generators installed, but in most cases,

when you hear the term "generator" in a modern turbine aircraft, assume it refers to an AC generator.

It's important to note that an electric motor is simply the opposite of a generator. In a motor, electricity passing through a coil creates an electromagnet that interacts with fixed magnets to rotate a shaft. In many smaller turbine installations, each engine's generator also serves as a starter motor. With this type of starter/generator, the distinction lies simply in whether the device is being electrically driven by a battery (or another power source) to spin the engine, or mechanically driven by the engine to generate electricity.

Types of generators

Many aircraft manuals use the term "Integrated Drive Generator" (IDG) when discussing the aircraft's generator. An Integrated Drive Generator is simply a generator connected to a Constant Speed Drive (CSD) unit that acts as an automatic gearbox to maintain a constant AC output frequency from the generator, regardless of the engine RPM. The main drawback of this type of generator is the high weight of the CSD gearbox.

IDG (integrated drive generator)

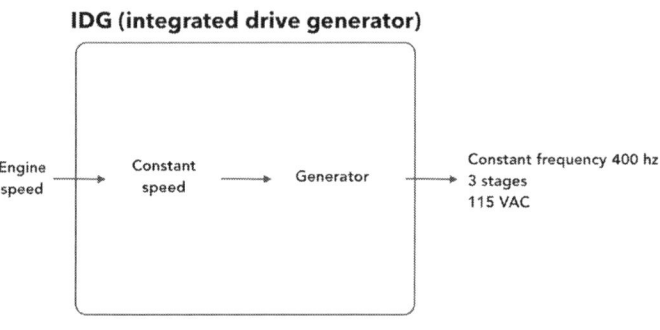

Although uncommon, it's possible for an Air-cooled Integrated Drive Generator (IDG/CSD) to overheat and trigger a warning message or caution light in the cockpit. When this happens, the flight crew can disconnect the generator from the engine accessory drive by activating an IDG/CSD disconnect switch on the electrical panel. Once disconnected in flight, the generator can only be reconnected on the ground by maintenance personnel. For this reason, most IDG/CSD switches have a protected cover secured with safety wire to prevent inadvertent activations.

Some aircraft use a Variable Speed Constant Frequency (VSCF) generator. With this system, the AC output frequency of the generator is allowed to increase and decrease with changes in engine RPM, sometimes referred to as "wild frequency." Instead of using a heavy CSD gearbox to mechanically drive the generator at a constant RPM and produce a constant frequency, VSCF systems use electronic power control units to convert the variable frequency output to a usable standard constant frequency (e.g., 400 Hz).

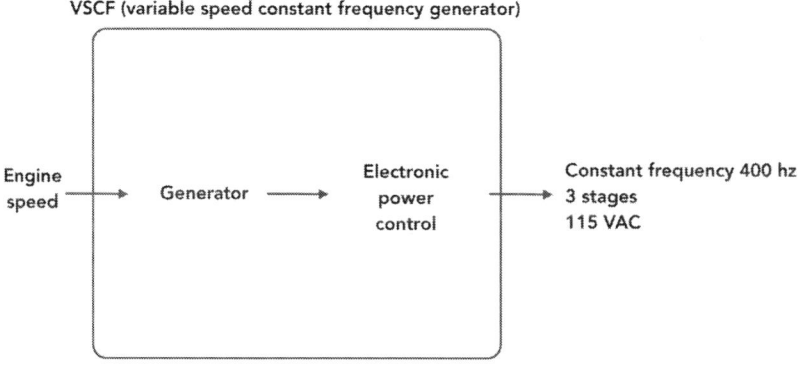

VSCF (variable speed constant frequency generator)

Engine speed → Generator → Electronic power control → Constant frequency 400 hz 3 stages 115 VAC

Newer aircraft and business jets use Variable Frequency Generators (VFG) instead of traditional constant frequency power sources. These generators are directly coupled to the engines and supply variable AC frequencies ranging from 360 to 800 Hz depending on engine speed.

Variable frequency generator systems offer distinct advantages over their predecessors, such as reduced weight, increased reliability, and higher efficiency. Additionally, power generated by such systems can be directly consumed by devices not sensitive to frequency, such as galley equipment and electric de-icing systems. Devices requiring a constant electrical frequency are supplied by dedicated electronic power control units associated with VSCF generators. Devices requiring DC are supplied by transformer-rectifiers.

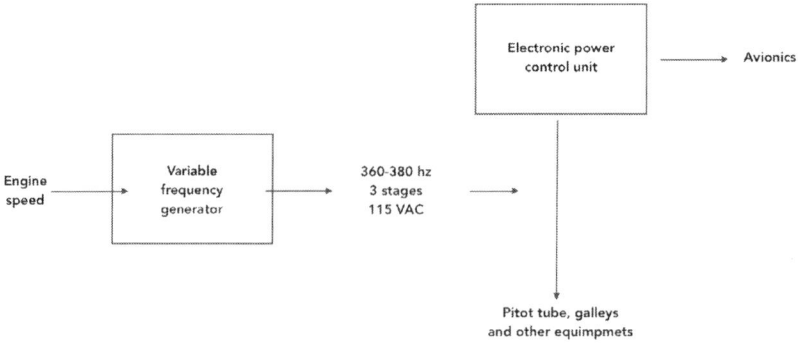

Battery

The battery can be considered as an energy reservoir that stores electrical energy in chemical form. Energy must be sent to the battery from another source (the aircraft generator). The battery can then act as a power source itself until the stored energy is depleted. Once charged, a battery will supply a circuit with voltage and current for a limited period of time. Consequently, batteries are rated in volts and ampere-hours.

Often people are confused as to why the voltages of the battery and the generator are not the same in a given system. In an electrical system, the generator voltage must exceed the battery voltage to charge it. Therefore, the battery voltage is always slightly lower than the generator voltage in a given system. (The battery is normally rated slightly above 24V in a 28V system.)

The battery's ampere-hour ratings simply indicate how many amperes the fully charged battery is designed to provide over a certain period. If you want to know how long your battery will last after a generator failure, simply sum the loads, in amperes, of the operating electrical components and divide by the battery's ampere-hour rating. For example, a fully charged 30 ampere-hour battery will theoretically supply 30 amperes for one hour, 15 amperes for two hours, or 60 amperes for half an hour. To conservatively determine the component loads, simply sum the amperage ratings stamped on the circuit breakers (CBs) of the operating components. You might be surprised at how little reserve is left in the battery.

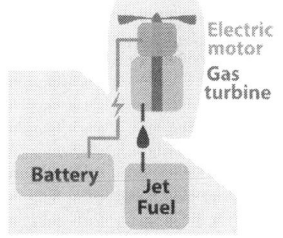

International regulations require thirty minutes of available operation on battery power. However, this is based on properly reduced electrical loads and a new, fully charged battery. You can see that in the event of a total generator failure, it requires skill and perhaps some luck to quickly identify the battery reserve, descend, and land before losing the entire electrical system. In addition to storing energy, batteries have another practical feature. A battery acts as a buffer in a circuit because it can absorb a power surge or "spike" that might otherwise damage circuit components.

The generators and battery power, through many circuits, all the aircraft's electrical devices and systems, including lighting, avionics, electric motors, and many flight instruments. While circuits can normally be powered by either the generator or the battery, the battery does not provide enough power over time to be useful as the sole source of electrical power. In fact, in large aircraft, many electrical devices cannot be operated when only battery power is available. The generators effectively power everything during flight, while the battery acts only as a reservoir and buffer. The same typically occurs at the gate: ground power from an AC plug, an Auxiliary Power Unit (APU), or a Ground Power Unit (GPU) powers the aircraft systems and keeps the battery charged.

Most smaller turbine aircraft engines are started using electric starters or starter/generators. A significant amount of electrical power is required to start a turbine engine. During approximately half a second, an average turbine engine start can require nearly 2,000 amperes. Therefore, a battery start necessitates a battery in excellent condition. Since weak batteries can cause a hot start, it is necessary to verify the battery's condition before each attempt. (Weak batteries cause hot starts because they fail to properly spin the engine's compressors.)

Typically, the minimum battery voltage for a battery start is around 22V in a 28V system. Otherwise, the pilot should request a Ground Power Unit (GPU) for assistance with the start. Many turbine operators use GPUs for starting whenever available to reduce wear on their expensive engines and batteries.

Types of batteries

In turbine aircraft, two different types of batteries are commonly found. Smaller turboprops usually have the same basic type of lead-acid battery found in piston aircraft and automobiles. Increasingly, turbine aircraft are equipped with nickel-cadmium (Ni-cad) batteries. Ni-cad batteries are much more expensive than lead-acid models, but they have some distinct advantages. They maintain a constant voltage over a longer period, whereas lead-acid batteries tend to drop off more quickly. Ni-cad batteries recover quickly after heavy use and can also supply a

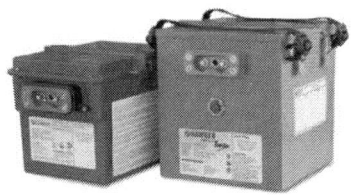

large amount of current. Since a weak battery can cause a damaging hot start of the engine, many operators find Ni-cads worth the additional investment.

However, Ni-cad batteries also have some disadvantages compared to lead-acid batteries. One of them is the memory effect. If a Ni-cad battery is almost always kept fully charged, it tends to lose some of its capacity to handle more demanding situations. For example, if ground power units (GPUs) are used for every start over several months, the battery becomes accustomed to providing only limited power and then recovering in a short time.

It may then be unable to supply enough power for a battery start. When this happens, the battery must be removed for maintenance and subjected to a deep discharge. This refers to the process of completely discharging the battery and then slowly recharging it with a trickle charger. (Do you use a rechargeable razor or flashlight? These also have Ni-cad batteries, so you can experiment with battery memory and deep discharge principles.) You can see that good preventive maintenance involves performing battery starts at least periodically to exercise the battery.

Finally, Ni-cad batteries are sometimes subject to a phenomenon called "thermal runaway" (sometimes also known as "battery runaway"). Thermal runaway occurs when excessive current is drawn from the battery and then recharged. The battery overheats and begins to self-destruct. Unless addressed in time, sometimes the overheating cannot be stopped until the battery is completely physically destroyed. Some aircraft have battery temperature indicators in the cockpit to detect this condition, while in other cases, only electrical tests can be performed by the pilots.

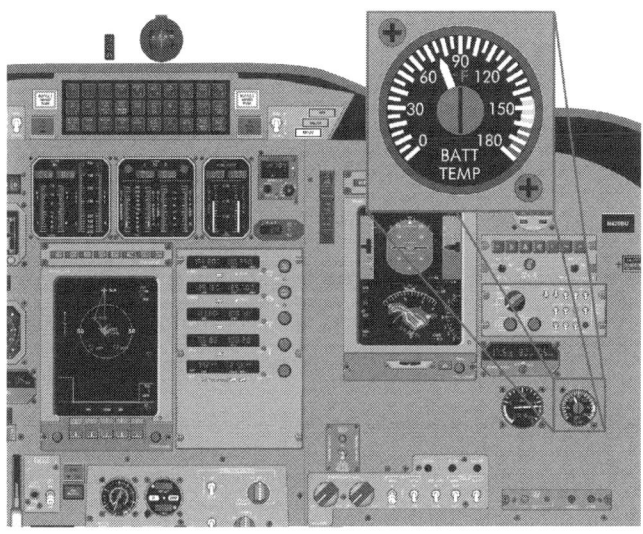

In any case, thermal runaway can be a very serious problem. The procedure involves immediately isolating the battery from all other circuits and making an immediate landing. Runaway batteries can potentially damage other electrical components, cause fires, and damage the aircraft's structure due to the release of internal battery chemicals. In some cases, a runaway battery can, in extreme circumstances, burn through its compartment and fall out of the aircraft.

Control devices in each electrical circuit regulate the electricity to operate aircraft systems and components. Manual switches range from simple on/off switches for lights and radios to master aircraft and avionics switches that control electrical power to many different items simultaneously. Rheostats adjust the electrical flow to variable devices like instrument lights. Remote mechanical switches are used for purposes such as limit switches (e.g., to shut off the flap motor when the flaps are fully retracted) and squat switches (to confirm, when closed, that the landing gear is down and weight is on the wheels).

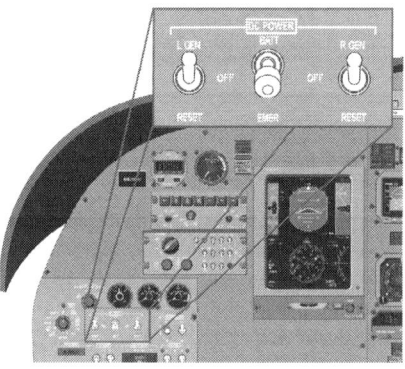

Relays and solenoids are remotely or automatically controlled switching devices built around electromagnets. In each device, a small amount of current is sent through a coil to move a switch or shaft. Relays are used to remotely control electrical circuits carrying large amounts of current. (Newer solid-state devices are replacing relays in many applications.) A solenoid is also a remotely electrically powered control device but is designed to move a shaft over a short distance when energized. Solenoids are used to remotely operate hydraulic and pneumatic valves, as well as small mechanical devices and other switches.

Relays, solenoids, and associated devices are very important in modern aircraft due to the trend towards computerized systems. They enable the remote electronic control of all types of aircraft systems, whether hydraulically, pneumatically, or electrically powered.

Electrical conversion devices

Today, most larger turbine aircraft require a variety of different types of electrical power. While a navigation light or a radio requires little system power to operate, the consumption of a flap motor can be enormous. To adequately meet these varied needs, different types of electrical power are required. Many general-use items operate on 28V direct current (DC). Alternating current (AC) often powers high-consumption items in larger aircraft.

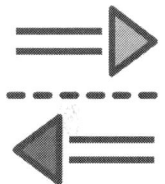

A series of electrical conversion devices is required to match the variable power requirements of the aircraft's electrical components to the available sources. Transformers are used to adjust the system voltage (usually down) for specific applications. Transformer-rectifier units (TRUs) convert AC generator output to DC.

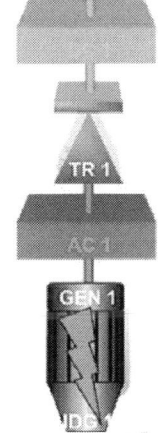

Some electrical flight instruments, such as gyroscopes and some engine instruments, often operate on low-power 26V AC. Inverters convert DC to AC for this purpose. (Incidentally, AC-powered instruments fail differently than DC-powered instruments. The old saying is "AC lies, DC dies." While a DC meter goes to zero when power is disconnected, an AC needle freezes in place where it was when power was lost.)

Bus bar system

The main safety feature of sophisticated aircraft electrical systems is redundancy. Multiple power sources are used, each protected against the failure of the others and capable of powering a wide and overlapping variety of equipment. This is achieved through the use of a bus bar system, meaning that the aircraft's electrical system is carefully organized into a set of separate but interconnected circuits. Bus bar systems allow critical circuits to be isolated from each other and supplied with power through alternative sources in the event of a failure.

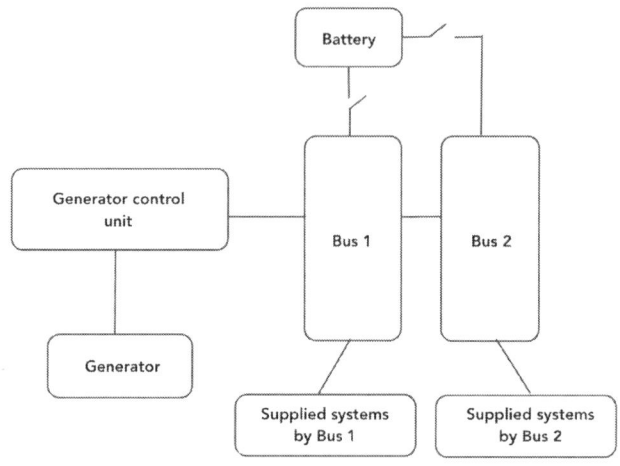

A bus bar system is configured so that each power source supplies one or more specific bus bars. Each bus bar can be thought of as an electrical hub, with various components connected to it for power. The bus bars are interconnected through some type of circuit protection device so that, in the event of a bus failure, other bus bars are instantly disconnected to prevent them from also being affected. Additionally, a bus bar that has lost its normal power source due to a failure can often receive power alternatively through another source via another bus bar.

Let's see how bus bars are configured to provide protection through redundancy. If two critical safety systems of the aircraft back each other up, each will be located on a separate bus to avoid the simultaneous loss of both due to an electrical issue.

For example, each engine-driven generator normally powers its own "generator bus," on which the highest-draw items in the aircraft are typically found. Redundant items are divided between the buses. The pilot's windshield heater and the co-pilot's rear window heater might be powered from the left generator bus, while the co-pilot's windshield heater and the pilot's rear window heater are on the right generator bus. This way, if one of the generator buses fails under icing conditions, someone should still be able to see through the windshield to land.

Items such as built-in fire extinguishers and emergency lights are usually powered from a "hot battery bus." This way, they have power for use even when no generator power is available and all switches are off. A "battery bus" is typically powered by the aircraft's master switch so that radios, lighting, and some other items can operate on the battery when the engines are not running. You can see why the electric windshield heater wouldn't be on that bus—it would drain the battery in minutes, and who needs it when on the ground?

Most aircraft systems are configured so that battery buses can be powered by generators if the battery fails in flight. Some generator buses can also be selectively powered by the battery, but not for long (the electrical demands are too high).

Protective devices

A variety of devices are used to protect system components from damage due to failures. Resettable circuit breakers (CBs) automatically disconnect when individual components are drawing too much current. It is important to know the procedures for resetting them in each aircraft. In some aircraft, pilots are advised not to reset CBs except in emergencies. More commonly, a CB is reset only once and then left as is. Incidentally, a CB disconnects when its casing expands due to heat. If it has not cooled down, it will not reset, even if the component is fine. Wait a few moments before attempting to reset them.

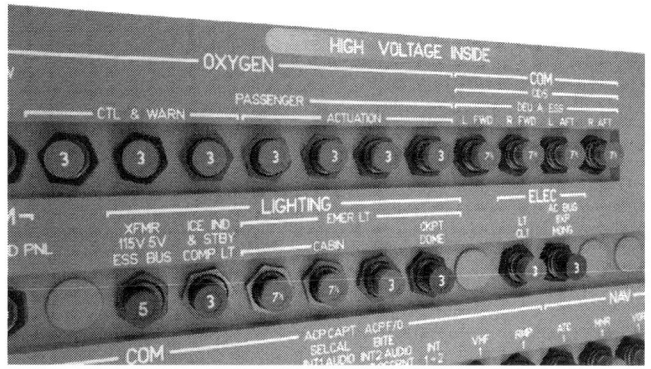

Current limiters and fuses can also be used to open circuits that are drawing too much current. They can isolate specific components or one bus from another. Unlike CBs, they cannot be reset and generally must be replaced by maintenance personnel after opening their circuits. Most fuses blow almost instantly, but in some cases, slow-blow fuses or current limiters are used when higher-than-normal current is needed for short periods (e.g., during engine start cycles).

Diodes function as check valves in a water system; they allow electricity to flow in only one direction through a circuit, thus protecting components "upstream" from electrical flow in the wrong direction.

Electronic circuit protection devices include a wide variety of automatic sensors and computer-controlled switching systems. Among the most common are the generator control units (GCUs) mentioned earlier, which protect generators and their associated buses from failures. Hall effect devices are sometimes used to protect against unidirectional current overloads, typically between buses.

Some aircraft, like the Dash-8, have sophisticated computer bus bar protection units that electronically monitor and protect the entire bus bar electrical system from failures.

Bus bar connections are switches or relays used to connect or disconnect bus bars from each other. They serve to isolate failed buses from those that are functioning correctly and can be operated manually or automatically, depending on the specific aircraft installation. Bus bar connections are also used to reroute electrical power to buses that have lost their normal power sources.

Emergency electrical generator

As discussed earlier in the battery section, for a battery system to be considered airworthy, it must provide at least thirty minutes of emergency electrical configuration to power essential items. However, turbine-engine aircraft often conduct longer-range operations where thirty minutes of electrical backup may be insufficient. Moreover, turbine-engine aircraft have higher electrical loads and more demanding flight environments than the light piston aircraft many of us trained in. Therefore, most turbine-engine aircraft are equipped with emergency power generation systems.

An Auxiliary Power Unit (APU) is a small turbine engine usually located in the tail of an aircraft and designed to provide supplementary electrical power as needed. In emergency situations, most APUs can be started in-flight and operated as long as necessary to supply the required electrical power until a safe landing is made.

Many APUs can handle the entire electrical load of an aircraft without assistance from the main engine-driven generators.

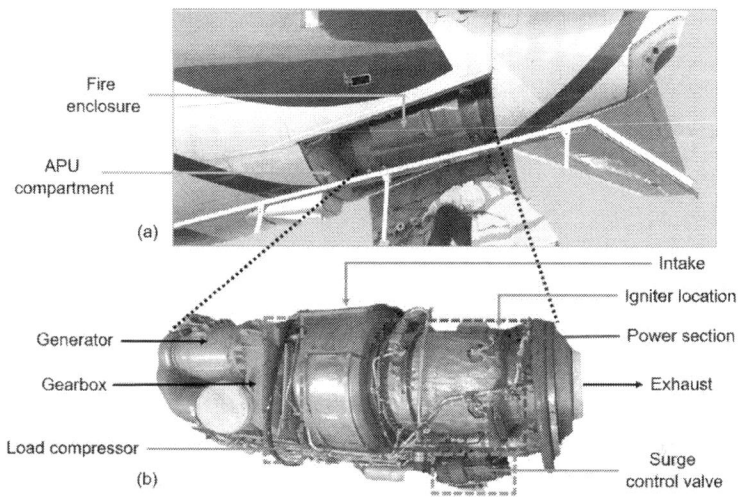

Engine-driven backup generators can also be installed near, but independently of, an aircraft's main electrical generators. The most common system uses a variable frequency generator as an electrical backup source in the event of main engine-driven generator failure.

A hydraulic motor generator (HMG) or hydraulically driven generator (HDG) is simply an electrical generator driven by hydraulic fluid under pressure from a hydraulic pump, rather than being mechanically driven directly by an engine. In concept, the HMG performs the opposite function of an electrically driven hydraulic pump, similar to our earlier discussion on starter/ generators. Instead of electrical power driving the hydraulic pump, the hydraulic pump drives the generator producing electrical power.

Typically, an HMG is only used after the loss of the aircraft's main electrical power generators, generating enough power to supply most of the captain's side of the cockpit, including the flight management computer and electronic flight displays.

An emergency air turbine (RAT) can also be used to generate emergency electrical power in the event of a total loss of the engine-driven main generators. A RAT is an air-driven turbine usually located on the aircraft's fuselage underside. In the event of a complete loss of engine-generated electrical power, the RAT can be automatically or manually deployed into the aircraft's airstream, where it will start spinning, generating enough electrical power to supply emergency loads such as the captain's backup navigation and essential flight instruments.

Hydraulic system

The extensive hydraulic systems found in large aircraft may be entirely unfamiliar if you have been flying smaller, more recent model piston-engine planes or light turboprops. The only hydraulic systems generally found in those smaller vehicles are simple brake systems and, in some aircraft, self-contained "power pack" hydraulic systems for landing gear extension and retraction. Hydraulic systems are based on the simple principle that fluids are flexible but incompressible. Suppose you have a long tube filled with fluid. If force is applied to the fluid at one end of the tube, that force is transmitted, practically without loss, to the other end.

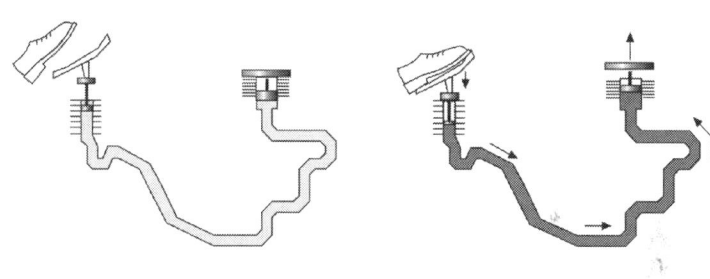

This can be illustrated at a basic level by considering a basic brake system such as that found in a light twin-engine airplane (or even a Cessna 152, for example). The power transmission requirement is straightforward. The pressure created by the force of your foot must be transmitted to the disc brakes on the wheels to stop the airplane.

This could have been achieved using cables and levers, but as early automobile manufacturers learned, cables stretch, and mechanical linkages wear out over time. Additionally, due to mechanical friction, much of the force applied by your foot is lost before it reaches the brakes. Furthermore, a heavy and complex linkage is needed to direct the mechanical force around all those bends between your foot and the brakes.

The solution is hydraulic brakes. A simple piston in the master brake cylinder under your foot applies force through a frictionless and flexible brake line to a similar piston in the slave cylinder of the brakes. The slave cylinder then converts hydraulic pressure into mechanical force to compress the brake caliper. By controlling the sizes of the master and slave cylinders, designers can establish a proportional mechanical advantage. That's why you can stop an airplane weighing thousands of pounds with just the pressure applied by your feet.

In larger aircraft, the hydraulic system provides a powerful yet relatively lightweight transmission method. Instead of using high-current electric motors and heavy mechanical drive trains to operate each flap, landing gear, and spoiler, a hydraulic pump can transfer electric or engine power through a hydraulic system to control everything.

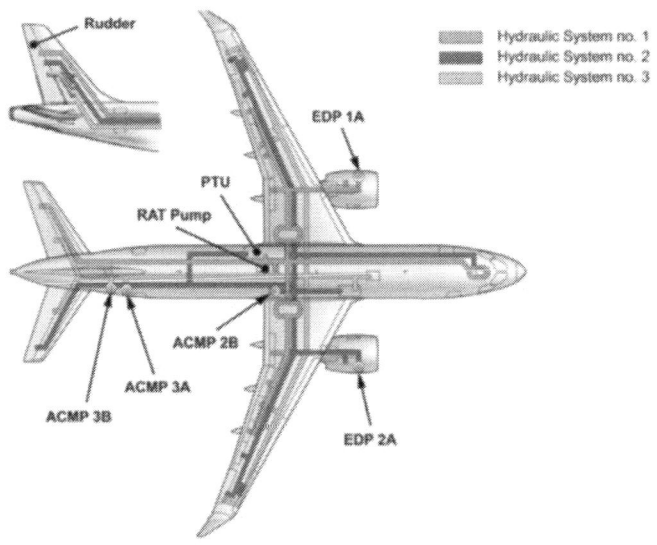

Hydraulic System no. 1
Hydraulic System no. 2
Hydraulic System no. 3

Hydraulic power is especially valuable for heavy-duty applications because it can be drawn directly from engine power without overloading the aircraft's electrical systems. Electric motors draw enormous current when used for intermittent heavy-duty operations. That's why all the cabin lights dim when you electrically operate the landing gear in a small aircraft.

For these reasons, hydraulic power has proven to be more reliable and require less maintenance for heavy-duty applications than traditional electromechanical drive trains. An additional benefit is that, by requiring fewer and smaller electric motors, the aircraft's electrical systems can be lighter and last longer. Finally, an engine-driven hydraulic system provides another power source for redundancy in critical systems.

The hydraulic systems of aircraft operate at very high pressures, typically around 3,000 psi (pounds per square inch), and sometimes at high temperatures. Hydraulic fluids are specially formulated to withstand these conditions without evaporating. This is because the key characteristic that allows a hydraulic system to function is the incompressibility of the fluids. If the fluid evaporates in the line, it turns into a gas with completely different properties, potentially causing transmission efficiency loss or even "vapor lock" in small lines.

Most turbine-powered aircraft are designed with two or more completely separate hydraulic systems. For standardization, these hydraulic systems are designated with letters, numbers, or colors (for example, System A and System B or System #1 and System #2). These separate systems share the hydraulic workload and are designed so that one hydraulic system can support another in case a system pump fails or if one or more systems lose hydraulic pressure or fluid. Some aircraft incorporate dedicated reserve hydraulic systems for use when a primary system fails.

The Airbus A320 aircraft identifies its three hydraulic systems using colors.

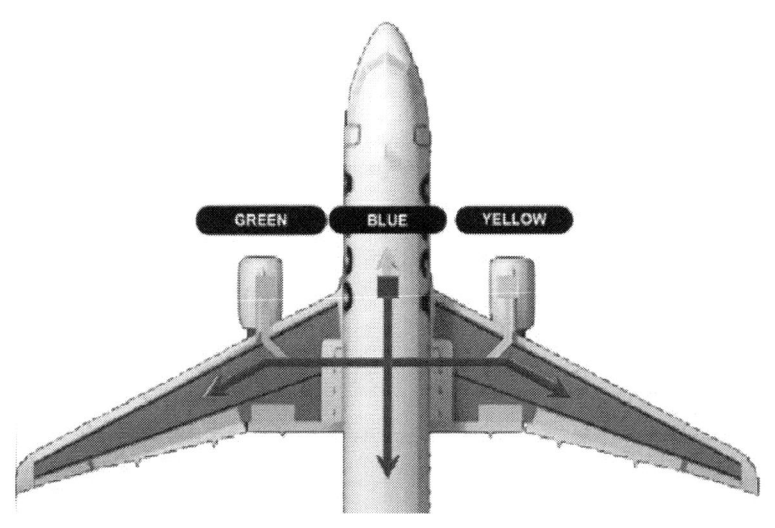

The Boeing B737 aircraft identifies its three hydraulic systems using letters.

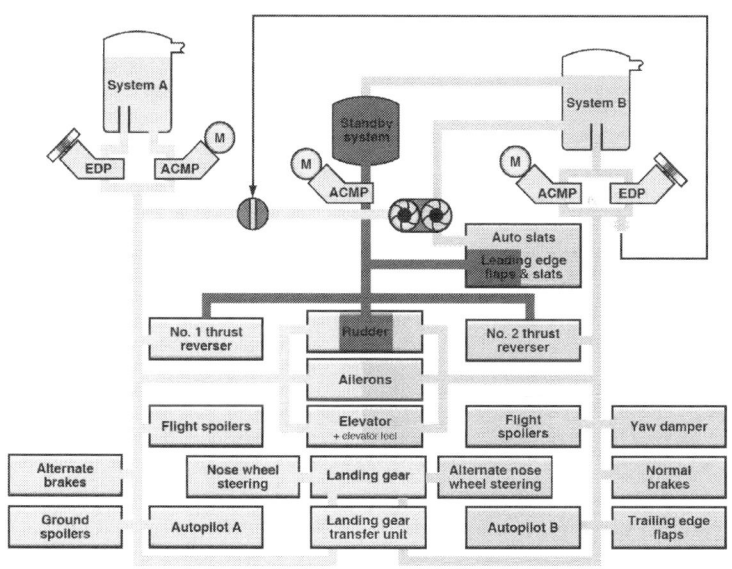

Hydraulic pumps in aircraft are typically rotary pumps, directly driven by the aircraft's engines or powered electrically. These pumps convert the rotary motion from the power source into hydraulic pressure and flow, which is then delivered to the mechanical systems of the aircraft through hydraulic lines. Pumps can be designed for continuous operation or periodic use. In larger aircraft, a pump driven by the engine is usually installed for each power plant, along with one or more electrically driven pumps for redundancy. Aircraft hydraulic systems are often interconnected, but with isolation valves installed to separate them. Each pump individually can typically supply most or all of the hydraulic demand of the aircraft. Some aircraft have reserve hydraulic pumps installed to support the main pumps in case of failure.

Hydraulic motors are relatively small units compared to electric motors, converting hydraulic energy back into mechanical energy. They are typically rotary units (essentially "inverted pumps") that convert hydraulic pressure and flow into rotary output to operate mechanisms such as flaps or landing gear.

Hydraulic cylinders use pistons to transform hydraulic pressure into linear mechanical motion. They are used for various purposes, with brake operation being one of the most obvious examples. Hydraulic cylinders are also employed to actuate control surfaces, landing gear doors, airstair doors, and other devices with relatively short travel.

Hydraulic lines, both flexible and rigid, transport hydraulic power from the pump to the hydraulic motor.

Valves direct the flow of hydraulic fluid, and thus power, to where it is needed. For example, in the case of hydraulic landing gear, valves can direct hydraulic flow/pressure to one side of the landing gear motor to retract it, or to the other side to extend it. Remember that the valve needs to receive instructions from the landing gear lever in the cockpit to correctly direct power. This activation requires energy to change the valve position.

A hydraulic fuse is a safety component designed to prevent catastrophic loss of hydraulic pressure. Hydraulic fuses are strategically installed throughout an aircraft's hydraulic system and are designed to detect faults such as faulty connections or ruptures in hydraulic lines. If a leak occurs in the lines or hydraulic subsystems, the hydraulic fuse prevents excessive fluid loss while allowing the remaining components of the hydraulic system to operate.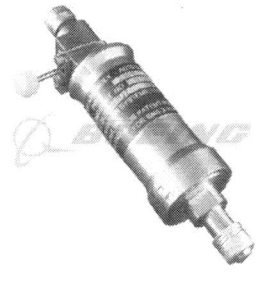

Typical designs of hydraulic fuses incorporate a spring-controlled mechanism that normally allows a certain volume of fluid flow per minute through the fuse. If the fluid flow through the fuse becomes excessive, such as in a rapid flow towards a rupture in the hydraulic line, the fuse closes to interrupt the flow, thereby isolating the area with the damaged line.

Hydraulic reservoirs

Hydraulic reservoirs are essential for holding the necessary amount of hydraulic fluid to operate aircraft systems, as well as serving as a reserve to compensate for potential leaks. Typically, low-pressure air is applied to the reservoir tanks to minimize foaming in the hydraulic fluid. Hydraulic accumulators store hydraulic pressure to provide backup during critical operations in the event of pump failure. They usually consist of a sealed pressure vessel with a diaphragm or piston installed.

The hydraulic pressure compresses nitrogen or "dry air" (and sometimes a spring) within the accumulator to store energy that can be used for a brief power application in case of pump failure.

Accumulators can also be used to control power fluctuations or overloads in the system, similar to a battery in an electrical system.

Hydraulic pump (backup)

The hydraulic systems of aircraft, as discussed, have a variety of designs. Common across all of them is the need for some form of backup system that provides hydraulic pressure to operate critical systems such as flight controls or landing gear when the main hydraulic pressure source has failed. These backup systems range from simple to complex, depending on the relative complexity of the hydraulic system itself. Smaller turbine-powered aircraft typically feature a manual hydraulic pump, used as a backup method to provide hydraulic pressure and extend the landing gear when the main pump fails. Most manual hydraulic pumps are either single-action (fluid moves during the power stroke but not during the return stroke) or double-action (fluid moves during both strokes).

During flight training in such aircraft, you will be required to manually extend the landing gear using the manual hydraulic pump. Many manual pumps require over 100 strokes to extend the landing gear, making emergency extension physically demanding and time-consuming. Therefore, do not attempt to manually extend the landing gear on final approach with such systems; climb to level flight at a safe altitude before performing emergency extension.

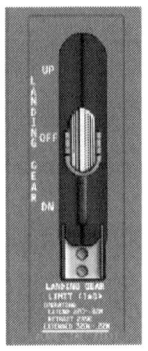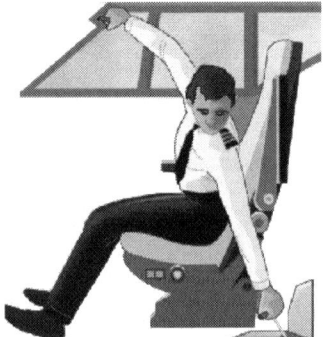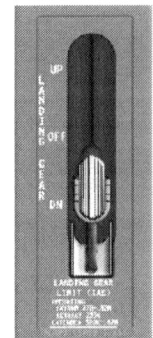

In larger turbine-powered aircraft equipped with engine-driven pumps as their main hydraulic pressure source, electric hydraulic backup pumps are used to supplement the main pumps and serve as emergency backup. Typically, electric hydraulic pumps can produce the same pressure as engine-driven pumps but with a much lower fluid volume. Therefore, operating high-load devices such as landing gear or flaps using backup pumps may take much longer than with normal engine-driven pumps.

Hydraulic power transfer units, found in more complex hydraulic systems, are hydraulically driven pumps that use pressure from one hydraulic system to pressurize another system. Usually, there is no exchange of fluid between systems, and electrical power availability is required to operate the unit. Hydraulic power transfer units are typically used as emergency backup for the engine-driven hydraulic pump.

Air turbine motor (ATM) hydraulic pumps use a large volume of compressed air from the pneumatic system originating

90

from a running engine, an auxiliary power unit (APU), or a ground air source to rotate an air turbine coupled to a hydraulic pump.

Emergency ram air turbines (RAT) can also be used to generate emergency hydraulic pressure in flight; they operate by extending an air turbine into the external airflow. Driven by impact air pressure, the turbine in turn drives a hydraulic pump, thereby providing emergency hydraulic pressure. RATs are typically found on aircraft that have only hydraulically powered flight controls, with no mechanical linkage between the cockpit controls and the flight control surfaces.

In the event of a complete hydraulic system failure, the RAT provides the necessary hydraulic pressure to operate the flight controls. To generate the required hydraulic pressure, the aircraft must fly at a speed high enough to generate sufficient air pressure to spin the air turbine. (For example, the Boeing 767 requires maintaining a minimum speed of 130 KIAS when using the RAT.) RATs are typically installed on the underside of the aircraft fuselage, where they can be easily deployed solely by gravity. RATs can be extended manually or automatically depending on the installation.

Characteristics of the hydraulic systems

One interesting characteristic of hydraulic systems is that most of the work is performed with very little movement. Continuous operation systems are constantly pressurized by hydraulic pumps, but fluid movement occurs only when a hydraulic component is in operation. Even then, fluid flow is minimal when feeding small actuators and cylinders. In these cases, work is done more through pressure than flow. We can liken a hydraulic system to a flexible rod pushed through a tube: a small movement at the driving end of the system is hydraulically transferred to press a distant button, move a valve, or deflect a control surface.

Since hydraulic pressure is contained between the pump and the devices it feeds, hydraulic return lines typically carry minimal flow or pressure back to the reservoir. Exceptions occur when rotary hydraulic motors are used to operate high-load devices such as landing gear and flaps. In those cases, both fluid flow and hydraulic pressure are significant.

Pneumatic system

The pneumatic system provides another method for transmitting engine power to various aircraft systems. In this case, the power transmission medium is compressed air. Since air, being a gas, is compressible, pneumatic power is much less efficient than hydraulic power for

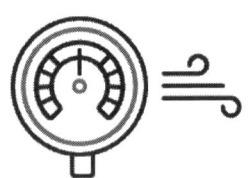

heavy-duty tasks. On the other hand, pneumatic systems are much lighter than hydraulic systems, require little maintenance, and do not need special fluids.

In piston aircraft, pneumatic power comes from mechanically driven pressure or vacuum pumps powered by the engines. These systems are essentially quite simple. Rotating pneumatic pumps correspond to the pump in our reference hydraulic power system. Atmospheric air source eliminates the need for any type of reservoir, and control is relatively straightforward through a series of valves. Pneumatic systems in piston aircraft typically operate gyroscopic instruments, pressurization, and de-icing boots.

Turbine aircraft use pneumatic systems for the same types of applications, and many more. The reason is that turbine engines are essentially giant pneumatic pumps. As you'll recall, the engine's gas generator compresses large amounts of air to support combustion. It's relatively straightforward to extract this "bleed air" from the engines and use it to power all sorts of devices.

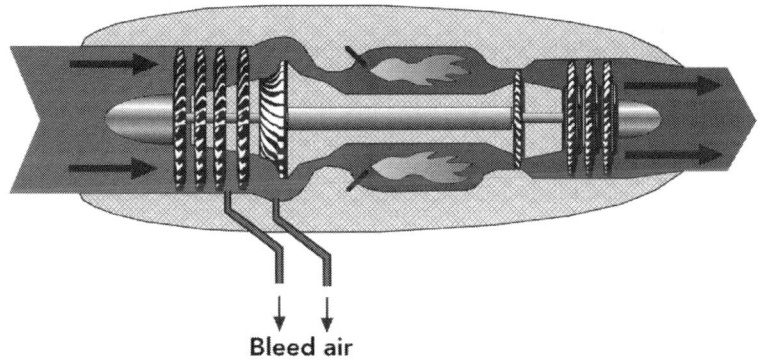

Bleed air

High-pressure bleed air is extracted from the compressor section of a gas turbine engine. Some systems extract bleed air from two or more 'stations' on each engine, resulting in different pressure and temperature outputs. These different bleeds are sometimes identified as 'high-pressure bleed air' and 'low-pressure bleed air.

High pressure air

High-pressure bleed air has many direct applications from the engine, including engine and wing thermal anti-icing. It is also used, through a combination of Air Cycle Machines (ACMs, or packs) and heat exchangers, for cabin pressurization, heating, and cooling. In large turbine aircraft, high-pressure bleed air also powers engine starters. Large engines like the CFM 56 are pneumatically started as an alternative to heavy electrical loads and the necessary motors for turbine engine electrical starting

Typically, for engine start, the Aircraft Auxiliary Power Unit (APU) is electrically started to provide bleed air pneumatic power, or a ground pneumatic power source is used. When the captain requests start, a start valve is opened, sending compressed air to spin a small turbine in the pneumatic starter. This, in turn, spins the engine's core compressor. Fuel is introduced, and when N2 (high-pressure compressor RPM) reaches a predetermined value, the start valve closes, and the starter turbine disengages from the engine compressor.

Low pressure air

Part of the high-pressure bleed air is regulated through a pressure regulator to much lower pressures, usually around 18 psi. This low-pressure air (sometimes called instrument air) corresponds, in pressure and applications, to the pneumatic (vacuum) systems of piston aircraft with which you may be familiar. As such, low-pressure air in turbine aircraft drives air gyroscopes and pneumatic de-icing systems, if installed. Low-pressure air can also be used for mechanical control functions, such as actuating valves (pneumatic and/or hydraulic), controlling pressurization outflow valves, and inflating door seals to maintain pressurization."

Dangers and Safeguards of Bleed Air

Since high-pressure bleed air is directly extracted from engines, its use in many turbine aircraft must be managed according to flight phase. For instance, bleed air usage affects the power output of the supplying engine as air and pressure are extracted from the engine before the combustion chamber. Therefore, in most turbine aircraft, the use of high-pressure bleed air is restricted during takeoff and approach situations. Low-pressure bleed air continues to operate during takeoff to power flight instruments, but other bleed-powered elements may be shut down for takeoff and then reactivated as part of the after-takeoff checklist, if applicable. Sometimes, weather conditions at takeoff necessitate the use of high-consumption bleed elements, such as engine inlet anti-ice systems. For these situations, most turbine aircraft have correction factors in their takeoff power and performance tables, which often restrict takeoff weights and/or speeds. The use of bleed air for thermal wing anti-icing is virtually never permitted during takeoff. Not only do bleeds consume significant engine power, but on the ground, bleed temperatures of 600° to 800°F can weaken the aluminum leading edges of the wings.

Bleed air pneumatic systems have associated hazards. Due to the high temperatures involved, fire can result from unmonitored bleed air leaks inside the aircraft. Therefore, bleed systems are typically monitored in the cockpit. Temperature probes are often used to monitor ducts carrying bleed air lines.

Other systems use pressurized tubing along bleed lines. This material melts and activates a sensor when a leak occurs. In the event of a high-temperature leak, the associated bleed source must be shut off, followed by execution of the corresponding 'abnormal' checklist. Some larger aircraft also have fire suppression capability for engine bleed lines in critical areas.

Pneumatic engine starting systems present their own interesting hazards. The pneumatic system pressure must be monitored throughout the starting cycle (described earlier) because if the start valve fails to close when the engine starts, high-pressure bleed from the running engine can backflow through the pneumatic starter. There have been several cases where a stuck start valve literally expelled the pneumatic starter from the aircraft, through the engine cowling, and a considerable distance from the aircraft. Therefore, engine start must be immediately aborted if the start valve fails to close when it should.

Like other aircraft systems, pneumatic systems have multiple power sources and protective devices to minimize system failure effects. Redundancy is achieved through the use of bleed sources from all engines and sometimes the Auxiliary Power Unit (APU) when installed. Check valves, similar to those found in our reference water system, are used to restrict pneumatic flow in certain areas in one direction.

Isolation valves (automatic or manual) allow separation of interconnected bleed systems in case of leaks or other failures. Typically, if a bleed at its origin is closed, most systems can operate on remaining bleed sources, except in high-consumption situations. However, if a serious leak occurs somewhere in the pneumatic system requiring the use of an isolation valve, some bleed-powered devices may become inoperative. For example, if there is a leak in the left-side low-pressure pneumatic system of your aircraft equipped with de-icing boots, you will first need to close the left bleed valve to prevent bleed air loss and engine/system power depletion. You will also need to isolate that side of the low-pressure system, likely resulting in a loss of some air-powered flight instruments and possibly some pressurization control functions.

Lastly, before using pneumatic de-icing boots, you must consider how they are affected. (Most modern aircraft allocate boots so that de-icing capability may be lost on some control surfaces, but not asymmetrically). Obviously, with this type of issue, you will want to land quickly in icing conditions. These are the types of scenarios you will need to memorize in ground school for your particular aircraft type."

Chapter 3

Fuel system

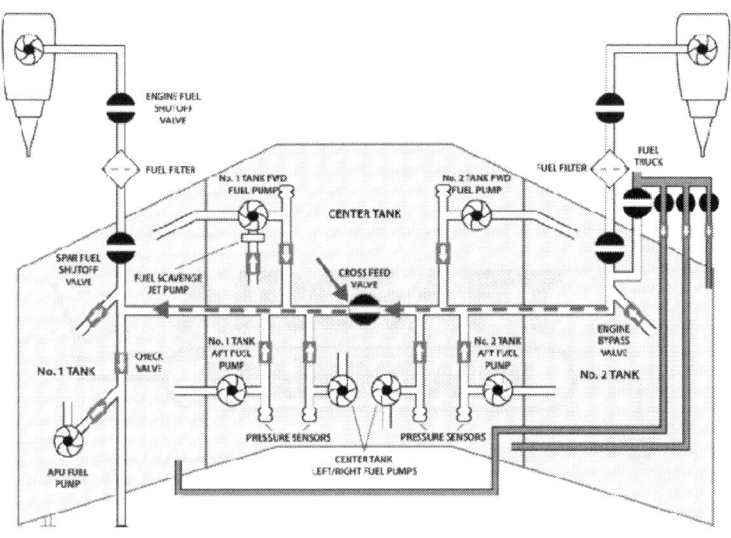

Introduction

The fuel system in any aircraft is designed to store fuel for flight and then supply it to the engines in appropriate quantities and at correct pressures. In turbine aircraft, this seemingly simple task becomes quite complex. Large quantities of fuel (often massive) must be  transported and distributed, multiple tanks and engines may be installed, and the characteristics of jet fuel and turbine engines themselves must be considered. Most civilian turbine aircraft fuel systems are designed for long-range operations and instrument flight rules (IFR) capability.

Fuel must be manageable during flight operations with an inoperative engine and, in some cases, must be shifted to maintain the aircraft within the center of gravity (CG) range. Therefore, most turbine aircraft fuel systems support fuel transfer between tanks and from one side of the aircraft to the other. As with every turbine aircraft system, redundancy is added for safety reasons.

Each aircraft has its own fuel system design, although in most cases they follow a similar operational diagram.

Diagrams of the fuel system of the Boeing 737 and Airbus A320 aircraft, respectively.

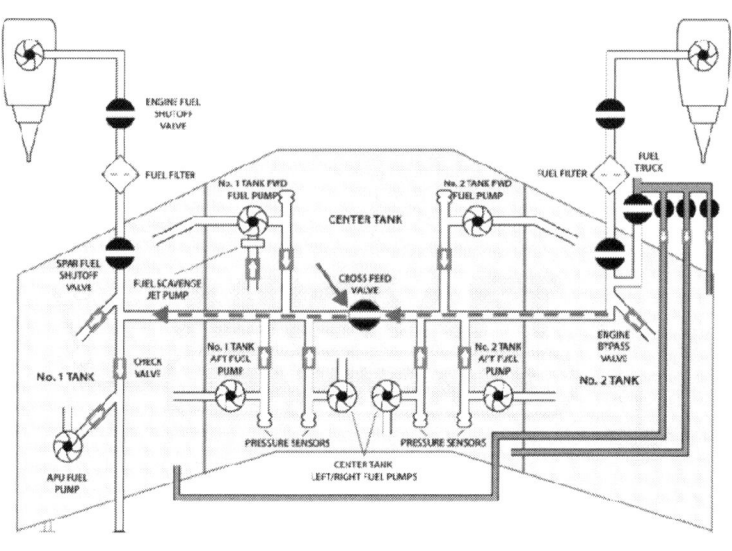

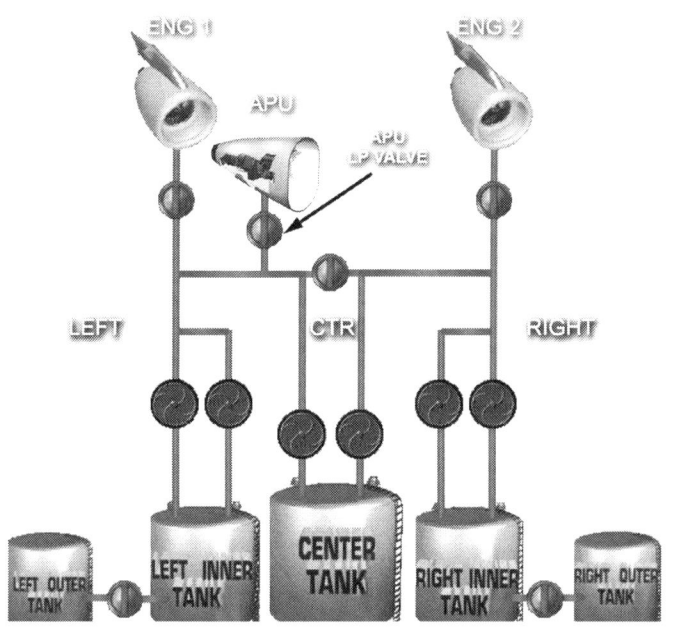

102

Fuel tanks

The increased complexity of a large turbine aircraft fuel system is immediately evident when considering the fuel tanks. Depending on the aircraft type, fuel tanks come in different sizes and shapes. They can be located in the wings, fuselage, and even in the tail.

Fuselage tanks are typically constructed of formed aluminum. However, most wing tanks are made by sealing part of the wing structure so it can hold fuel. These wet wings have largely replaced rubber tanks found in many older aircraft. External wing tanks, though not common in passenger aircraft, are quite prevalent in corporate aircraft. Tip tanks are found on some Learjets and Cheyenne turboprops, while the Lockheed Jetstar was equipped with underwing tanks.

Turbine aircraft engines can draw fuel from each tank separately, from interconnected fuel tanks, or from a main tank fed by a combination of reserve or auxiliary tanks. To ensure a constant fuel supply to the engines in all flight attitudes, fuel tanks are often divided or interconnected. Large turbine aircraft have long wings.

You can easily imagine that a fuel supply interruption to the engines could occur without a proper system design.

A common solution to this problem is the use of collector tanks. A collector tank is simply a separate segment of a larger fuel tank. It is located near the engine and supplies fuel directly to it. Each collector tank is in turn fed by selected regular tanks. In case of a momentary fluctuation in fuel supply from the regular tank, the collector tank takes over to provide continuous flow. One-way flapper valves (spring-loaded check valves) are sometimes installed between the collector tank and the rest of the fuel tank to prevent reverse flow into the main tanks.

Some aircraft are equipped with header tanks, which are small separate tanks that serve the same function as collector tanks. Other specialized fuel tanks are sometimes installed in aircraft for various purposes. Surge tanks, for example, are often found near the wingtips of large aircraft to control fuel movement, overflow, and venting.

Fuel components

In turbine aircraft fuel systems, a variety of pumps are installed to move fuel from tanks to engines and between tanks. The most common categories of fuel pumps include high-pressure pumps, low-pressure pumps, auxiliary pumps, and jet pumps.

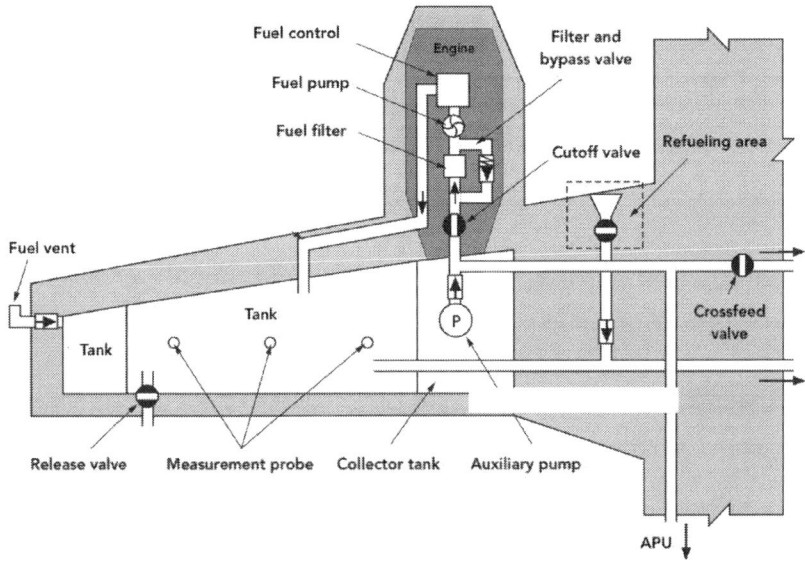

Fuel control

Engine

Filter and
bypass valve

Fuel pump

Fuel filter

Cutoff valve

Refueling area

Fuel vent

Tank

Crossfeed
valve

Tank

P

Release valve

Measurement probe

Collector tank

Auxiliary pump

APU

A high-pressure pump, driven by the engine, supplies fuel to each engine at pressures near 900-1,000 psi. High pressure is crucial for several reasons. Firstly, during takeoff, the fuel requirement can be two or three times higher than during normal cruise. Therefore, both pressure and flow capacity must be available to rapidly increase fuel delivery. (Excess fuel delivered by the pump at any given time is returned to the tanks via the return line.) High pressure also ensures adequate fuel delivery to the engine. Fuel is sprayed into the engine burner in an optimal pattern and pressure to optimize combustion, focus the flame in the combustion chamber, and prevent fuel injector overheating.

The low-pressure pump is typically also engine-driven. It draws fuel from the tanks and supplies it to the high-pressure pump, often through a fuel filter and heater.

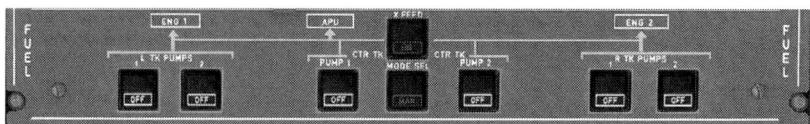

Most turbine aircraft fuel systems are also equipped with electric auxiliary fuel pumps. (These are also known as standby pumps, fuel transfer pumps, or boost pumps.) Auxiliary pumps serve various purposes depending on the specific aircraft fuel system design. They are often used to transfer fuel between tanks and to provide emergency backup to the engine-driven low-pressure pump. In large aircraft, boost pumps operate continuously in the tanks being used, as the suction from engine-driven low-pressure pumps may not be sufficient to extract fuel at altitude.

In most systems, auxiliary pumps are renowned for performing fuel transfers in the event of engine failure. Crossfeed refers to transferring fuel from tanks on one side of the aircraft to the engine(s) or tanks on the other side. It is an important safety feature in case of engine failure, allowing the operational engine to use fuel from the inoperative engine. Balancing fuel weight from one side to another can also be critical in such circumstances.

Most varieties of auxiliary pumps are operated from a fuel control panel located in the cockpit. (Auxiliary fuel control panels may be located on the wing for use by refuelers in larger aircraft equipped with single-point refueling systems.)

It's also noteworthy that turbine engines are quite versatile in terms of the fuels they can use. Many smaller engines, for example, are approved for limited use of gasoline. However, due to its lower lubricating qualities, the use of gasoline in fuel pumps is often restricted to just a few hours or the pumps must be rebuilt.

Another type of pumping action commonly found in turbine aircraft fuel systems is motive flow. Motive flow refers to the use of small venturi-type ports, which are used to suction fuel into collection lines. It's desirable to collect fuel from multiple locations in each tank to avoid supply interruptions and to back up any fuel intake blockages. Instead of installing many mechanically driven pumps throughout the tank, these venturi devices, or jet pumps, suction fuel into the lines by creating low-pressure areas in the fuel passing through the lines. Therefore, jet pumps cannot pump fuel on their own. Instead, they act as localized secondary pumps (sometimes called recovery pumps), effectively powered by the main line pump (usually the engine-driven low-pressure pump or an electric auxiliary pump).

Fuel valves

Various valves are used to manage the fuel flow. Most valves simply open to allow fuel flow or close to stop it. Check valves, like those in the reference water system, allow fuel to flow in one direction at multiple points in the system, but not in the other direction.

107

Fuel selector valves are used by pilots to allocate fuel supply to each engine from selected tanks. Cross-feed valves direct fuel from one side's tanks to engine(s) or tanks on the opposite side. (In some aircraft, cross-feed is authorized for emergency use only in case of engine failure. In other cases, cross-feed is approved for routine use to balance lateral fuel loads.)

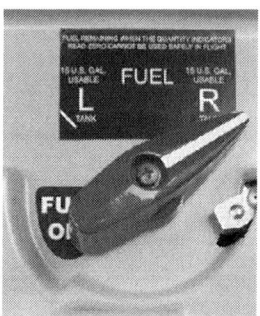

Fuel dump valves are installed on many aircraft where Maximum Takeoff Weight (MTOW) is significantly higher than Maximum Landing Weight (MLW). If an aircraft with a heavy load must return for immediate landing after takeoff, fuel is dumped overboard to reduce the aircraft's weight below MLW for a safe landing. (This fuel would typically have been consumed during the planned flight.)

All turbine-powered aircraft have some form of emergency fuel shut-off valve. Firewall fuel shut-off valves can be operated mechanically or electrically, depending on the manufacturer. These valves are used to cut off fuel supply to the engine section only during emergency engine shutdown. "Fire handles" (or "T-handles"), which operate firewall fuel shut-off valves, are one of the most visible controls in any cockpit.

Fuel heaters

Jet fuel unfortunately has the characteristic of absorbing water. When a turbine aircraft flies at high altitudes, the low temperatures of the outside air can cause this absorbed water to crystallize in the fuel system. As you can imagine, ice crystals clog the fuel filters and can accumulate to the point of causing an engine shutdown. (Engine shutdown means that combustion ceases in the engine: "the fire goes out"). Fuel heaters are used to warm the fuel and prevent this from happening. There are two common methods of heating the fuel: fuel-oil heat exchangers and fuel-air heat exchangers. Fuel-oil heat exchangers transfer heat from the engine oil to heat the fuel. Fuel-air heat exchangers use hot bypass air for the same purpose.

Fuel vent

Venting is crucial for the proper operation of any fuel system. As fuel is drawn from each tank, outside air must enter to replace it, or fuel flow will stop due to vacuum development. Simultaneously, fuel vents must also allow for the release of overpressure in the fuel tanks due to thermal expansion, but they must be designed to prevent fuel from venting to the outside under normal conditions. The delicate balance of fuel tank pressures is further complicated by the need for specialized vent designs in different locations. For instance, heated vents are used for structural ice protection, while flame arrestor vents protect fuel tanks from ignition by hot exhaust. Ram air vents capture impact air in flight to pressurize tanks and improve fuel flow.

Fuel control unit

The Fuel Control Unit (FCU) is a precise hydro-mechanical or electronically computerized device that supplies fuel to the engine. The FCU collects inputs such as throttle lever position, air pressure, and engine temperatures. It then meters the appropriate amount of fuel from the high-pressure fuel pump to the gas turbine engine combustion chamber. Different types of electronic fuel control units are sometimes known as "FADEC" (Full Authority Digital Engine Controls) or as "ECU" (Electronic Control Units). For redundancy, some aircraft have mechanical FCUs backing up ECUs in the same fuel system.

En the Boeing 737 aircraft, the fuel control unit is located on the overhead panel. From there, the pilot can operate the fuel pumps and the cross-feed valve or X-Feed. The fuel panel consists of two knobs on each pump that allow selecting them to ON or OFF. Above each pump, there are "low pressure" indicator lights. It has a rotary knob to open or close the cross-feed valve and an analog fuel temperature indicator. Additionally, it includes indicator lights for closed valves and fuel filter.

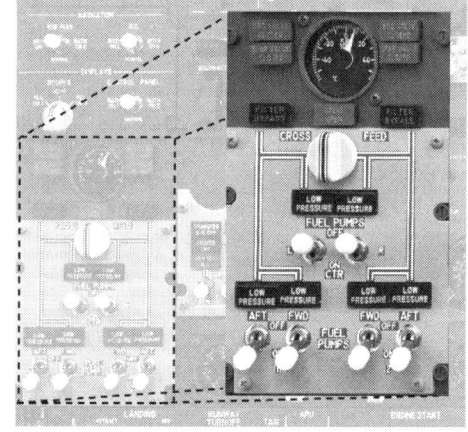

In the Airbus A320 aircraft, the fuel control unit is located on the upper panel. Let's now explore how the fuel system is operated from the control unit.

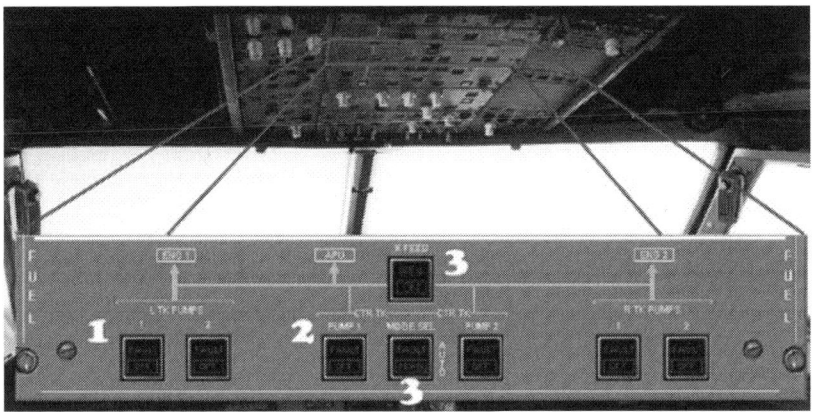

At point 1, it represents the operation buttons for the inner tanks' pumps, two on each side. At point 2, it represents the operation buttons for the central tank's pumps. Point 3 represents the cross-feed valve XFEED and just below it, a button known as the mode selector or MODE SELECTOR, which allows pilots to operate the central tank's pumps either manually or automatically, unlike the rest of the fuel pumps that are operated entirely manually. The APU does not have an activation or deactivation button for its fuel supply, as it is operated automatically upon starting the APU system.

Fuel measurement system

Fuel quantity indication systems are used to measure the mass of fuel (and thus the weight). These systems consist of a series of long metal probes that extend from top to bottom along the fuel

111

tanks. By measuring the electrical capacitance between the probes, the fuel quantity indication system determines the amount of fuel in one or more tanks. This information is sent to fuel quantity gauges in the cockpit, which of course display fuel in pounds. This type of system is easily calibrated to compensate for fuel movement within the tanks.

Fuel quantity indication systems are used to measure the mass of fuel (and thus the weight). These systems consist of a series of long metal probes that extend from top to bottom along the fuel tanks. By measuring the electrical capacitance between the probes, the fuel quantity indication system determines the amount of fuel in one or more tanks. This information is sent to fuel quantity gauges in the cockpit, which of course display fuel in pounds. This type of system is easily calibrated to compensate for fuel movement within the tanks.

To make life more interesting for you as a jet (or turboprop) aircraft pilot, ground fuel trucks typically measure fuel delivery in gallons due to their measurement systems. Therefore, when refueling, turbine pilots calculate their fuel needs for the next leg in pounds, but often request this fuel load in gallons. When precision is critical, a fuel conversion table can be used.

112

However, most of the time, fuel conversions are estimated at around 6.7 pounds per US gallon. The calculation and fuel ordering are often handled by the company dispatch in many scheduled carriers, relieving pilots of these calculations.

Sometimes it's desirable to physically measure the exact amount of fuel in a specific tank. (This may be for calibrating the aircraft's fuel quantity measurement system or to enable dispatch of the aircraft when a fuel gauge is out of service). Obviously, it wouldn't be practical to measure tens or hundreds of thousands of pounds of fuel in a large aircraft using manual dipsticks or five-gallon buckets. Therefore, many manufacturers incorporate relatively convenient mechanical measurement systems consisting of fuel quantity dipsticks.

These handy devices are used to measure fuel quantity from under the wings and are found in one or more hollow tubes that vertically traverse each fuel tank. Under normal circumstances, the dipsticks are locked in place in each fuel tank. To manually measure the fuel quantity, each dipstick is unlocked and lowered until its top is level with the fuel surface. In older "dipstick" models, the fuel level was identified when fuel began to drip from the bottom of the hollow dipstick.

Newer models, such as magnetic dipsticks, are found in sealed tubes. A magnetic float moves along the outer surface of each tube over the fuel. When the "Magnastick" is unlocked, it freely slides from the bottom of the wing until another magnet on the top of the dipstick aligns with the magnetic float. Both dipsticks and Magnasticks are calibrated so that the fuel quantity can be read directly, based on how much each dipstick protrudes from the wing."

Fuel management

A proper fuel management is crucial in turbine aircraft due to the large flows and weights of fuel involved, compounded by the specificities of each aircraft's fuel system. In many planes, tanks must be "consumed" in a specific order during flight, or excess fuel returning from the engine's high-pressure pump can inadvertently be pumped out.

Additionally, from a weight and balance perspective, improper fuel management can potentially create an unbalanced situation in many aircraft. These complexities necessitate that turbine pilots understand their fuel system, continually monitor fuel levels, and maintain a balanced fuel load.

With the addition of an aft fuel trim tank, current aircraft designs integrate fuel systems with aircraft center of gravity (CG) management to enhance performance. A fuel quantity and management computer controls necessary fuel load transfers. Fuel is transferred aft to move the aircraft's CG rearward and out of the trim tank to move the aircraft's CG forward. Fuel transfer to adjust the aircraft's CG leverages this phenomenon to reduce tail downforce and trim drag, allowing the aircraft to fly more efficiently.

Lateral fuel balancing has existed for many years. Fuel transfers in and out of the wing are used in many aircraft to reduce bending moments and thus structural fatigue in the wing structure. Consider the weight of all that fuel in the wing tanks. A Boeing 767 can hold 41,000 pounds of fuel per wing. On the ground, when there are no lift forces supporting the wing weight, a noticeable wing drop may sometimes occur when the wing tanks are full. By moving fuel to the inner tanks, we can minimize this effect.

Once the aircraft is airborne, lift curves the wings upward. Moving fuel to the outer tanks can also minimize this bending moment. In older aircraft, fuel load balancing was manually managed from a fuel control panel at the flight engineer's station. Newer aircraft automatically handle the complexity of fuel balancing using computerized systems.

Chapter 4

Engines of A320 and B737

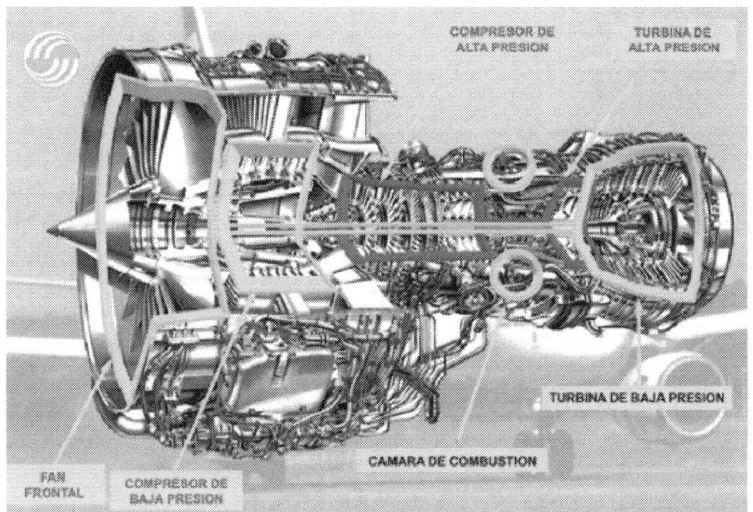

Introduction

With the purpose of becoming familiar with the different types of jet engines, this chapter analyzes the engine systems of two of the most flown aircraft in the world, the Airbus A320 and the Boeing 737.

Airbus A320 engine system

All aircraft in the A320 family are equipped with International Aero Engines (IAE) V2500 engines. Like most jet engines, our IAE is composed of:

- A low-pressure compressor.
- A high-pressure compressor.
- A combustion chamber.
- A turbine.

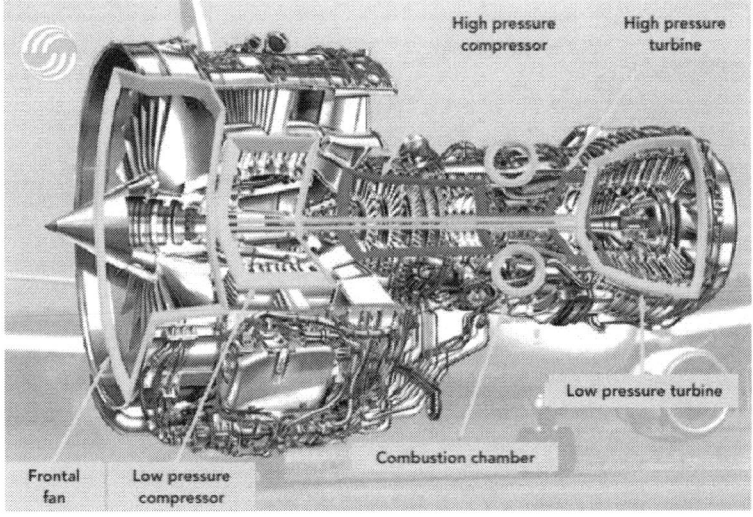

The low-speed rotor (N1) consists of a front fan and a low-pressure compressor connected to a low-pressure turbine, as shown in the following image:

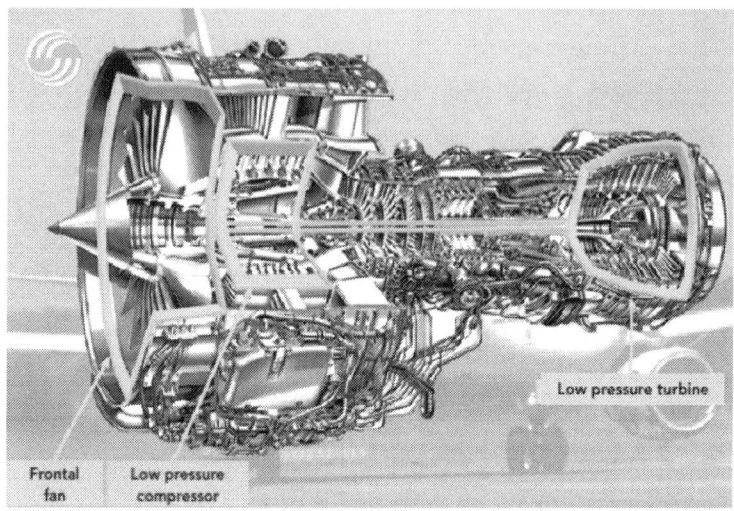

On the other hand, the high-speed rotor (N2) consists of a high-pressure compressor connected to a high-pressure turbine:

Lastly, the engine is equipped with a combustion chamber that has two ignition systems, ignition system A and ignition system B.

Each engine is equipped with a system called FADEC (Full Authority Digital Engine Control System), which manages all engine resources. It is a computerized system that not only monitors engine parameters but also optimizes engine performance.

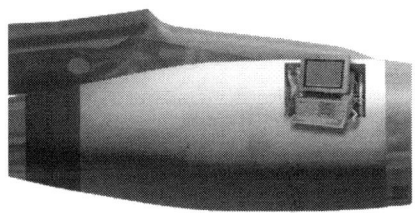

Each engine of the A320 is equipped with a reverser system, which is manually operated from the cockpit. It is a system that deflects the airflow, changing its direction to the opposite side to reduce engine thrust and thus decelerate the aircraft.

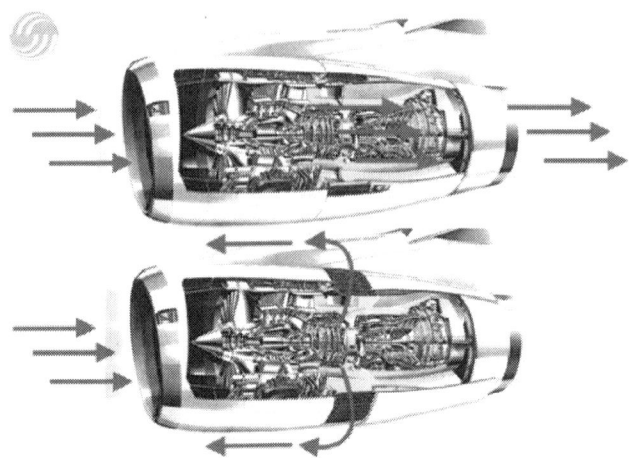

Now, let's move to the cockpit and see how the engines and reversers are operated by the pilots:

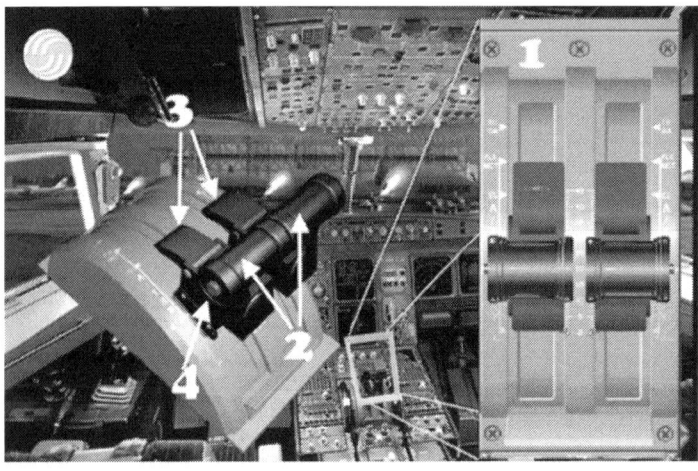

Located on the PEDESTAL panel, we find the throttle quadrant or thrust lever panel. It consists of two horizontally moving levers, forward and backward, used to increase or decrease engine power as required. In point number one, we see an overhead view of the throttle quadrant with its two levers and guides for their full range of movement. At point number two, we have the thrust levers.

Point number three indicates two plastic flaps that activate the thrust reversers when lifted and pulled backward. Finally, at point number four, there is a red button that disables the automatic thrust system known as AUTOTHRUST or A/THR.

Just below the throttle quadrant, we find the engine start panel. Let's see:

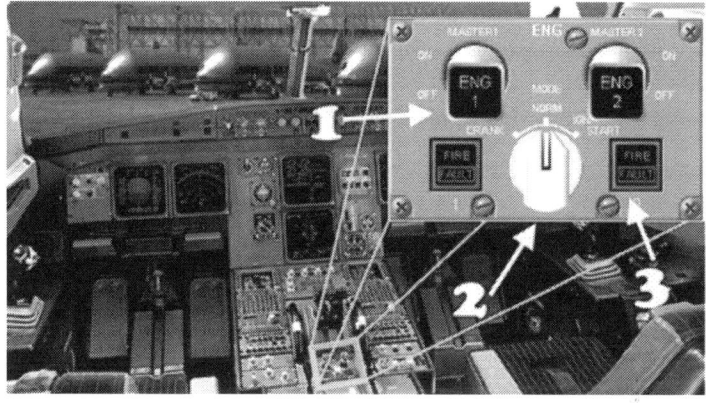

At point number one, there are two knobs indicating the number of each engine, known as the MASTER SWITCH for engine 1 and engine 2.

Point number two is a rotary knob with three positions: NORM for normal operation during flight, START to activate ignition system A or B in the combustion chamber, and CRANK to activate the engine drain system in case of a failed start.

Lastly, on the OVERHEAD panel, we find the manual start control panel in case of an unsuccessful automatic start.

Fuel system

The fuel system of our aircraft is similar to the traditional fuel system found in most airplanes. With its five tanks distributed between the fuselage and wings, the A320 has a capacity of 19,000 kilograms. The arrangement of its tanks is as follows:

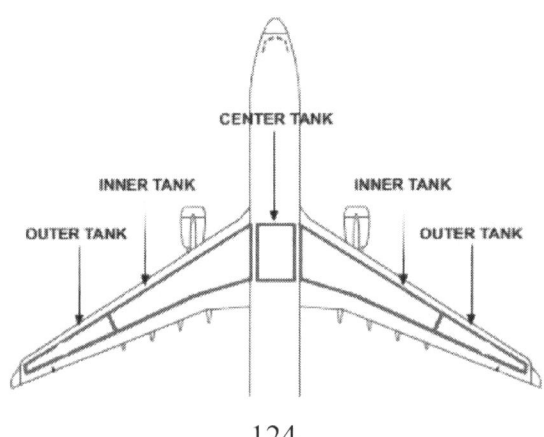

124

Except for the external tanks, the internal tanks and the center tank each have two fuel pumps and two transfer valves that connect the external tanks with the internal ones.

Fuel lines originate from the internal tanks and carry fuel directly to the engines, passing through two low-pressure valves that regulate the flow of fuel. The center tank also supplies fuel to the engines, but with only one pump for each engine. In the center conduit, there is a cross-feed fuel valve known as the XFEED VALVE. When this valve is open, the left engine is supplied with fuel from the right tank, and vice versa. The APU, on the other hand, is supplied with fuel from one of the pumps in the center tank and from the left tanks, both external and internal.

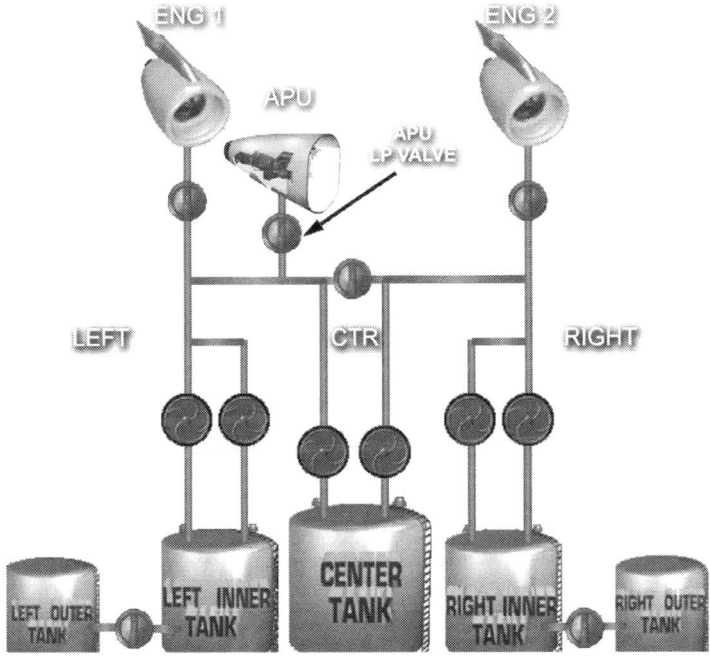

The above diagram depicts the architecture of the A320's fuel system. Let's see how it appears on the FUEL page of the ECAM and note the exact resemblance with its diagram:

At points 1, we have the five fuel tanks. At points 2, the two transfer valves. At points 3, the two fuel pumps for each tank. At points 4, the two low-pressure valves, one for each engine. At point 5, the XFEED valve. And at point 6, the APU valve.

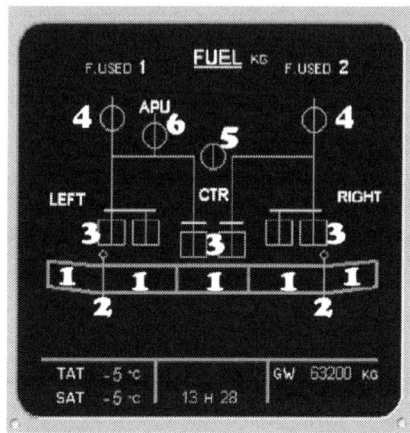

Now, let's observe the FUEL page on the ECAM and detail its information: Point 1 indicates the amount of fuel in kilograms available in each tank. Point 2 represents the temperature of the external and internal tanks. Point 3 indicates the fuel used by each engine. Finally, point 4 represents the FOB (Fuel on Board), which should match the sum of the quantities in each tank.

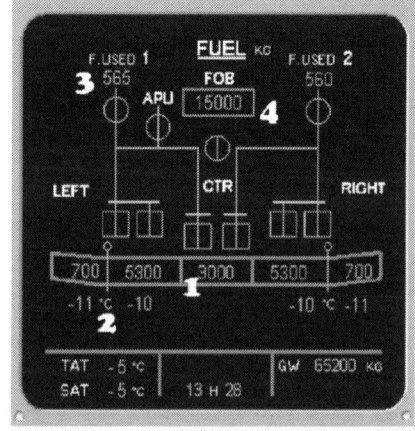

Now, let's understand how the fuel system is operated from the cockpit. Its panel is located on the OVERHEAD panel, like most systems. Let's see:

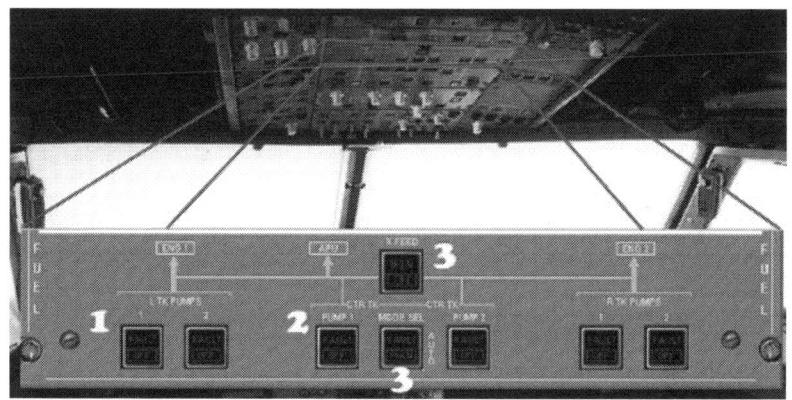

At point 1, we can see the operation buttons for the pumps of the internal tanks, two on each side. At point 2, we find the operation buttons for the pumps of the center tank. At point 3, on one side we have the XFEED, and just below it, a button known as the MODE SELECTOR, which allows pilots to operate the center tank pumps in manual or automatic mode, unlike the rest of the fuel pumps which are operated completely manually.

As we can see, the APU does not have an activation or deactivation button for its fuel supply, as it is operated automatically when starting the APU system.

127

The Autothrust system (A/THR) has the capability to operate in two different modes: Speed mode and THR mode.

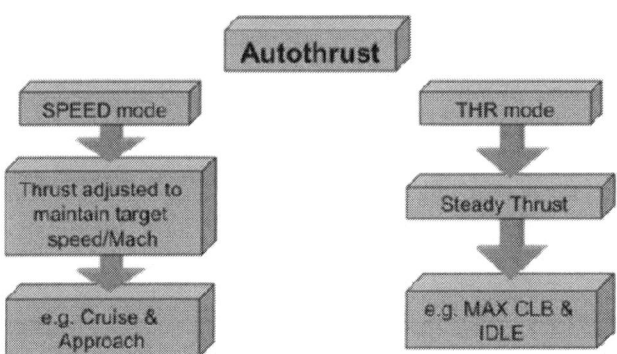

In SPEED mode, the system continuously adjusts thrust to maintain the target speed selected by the pilots, typically during cruise and approach phases. On the other hand, in THR mode, the system sets a specific thrust level without considering the previously selected speed. This mode is usually used during climbs (CLB) and when operating in IDLE.

Regarding the thrust levers, they have different positions corresponding to the available modes of the A/THR system. It starts at IDLE, in THR mode, where the engines produce minimum thrust to maintain taxi speed. Next to the levers, there are markings indicating the position of the thrust levers (arrows).

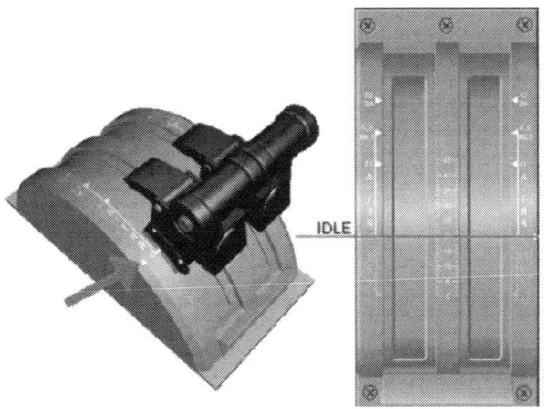

The second position after IDLE is CLIMB (CLB). This position corresponds to the SPEED mode of the A/THR system and is typically used during climb, cruise, descent, and approach phases.

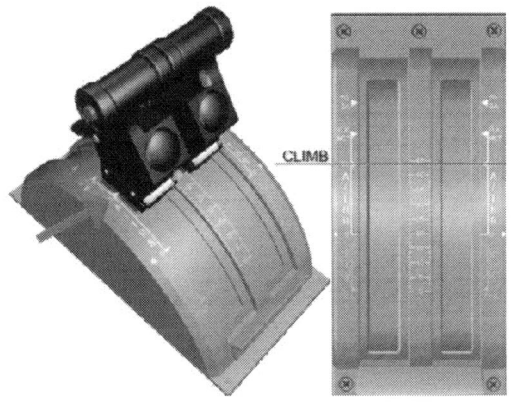

Lastly, there are two positions, MCT/FLX and TO/GA, used specifically during takeoff and go-around phases, depending on various factors such as:

- Meteorological conditions.
- Runway conditions.
- Aircraft weight.
- And during a go-around, in any situation requiring such a procedure.

In the MCT (maximum continuous thrust) position, the system uses the maximum available thrust continuously, typically used during engine failure procedures.

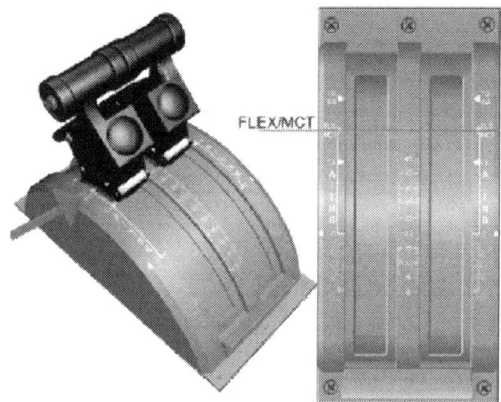

Additionally, this position also includes the FLEX position for temperature-limited takeoffs. The system uses the exact and necessary power for takeoff considering all the aforementioned variables. This approach preserves engine life.

Finally, the TO/GA (Take Off/Go Around) position is the maximum thrust position of the engines. It's typically used during maximum weight takeoffs or contaminated runways, and during a go-around procedure to ensure maximum climb rate immediately with the current aircraft configuration.

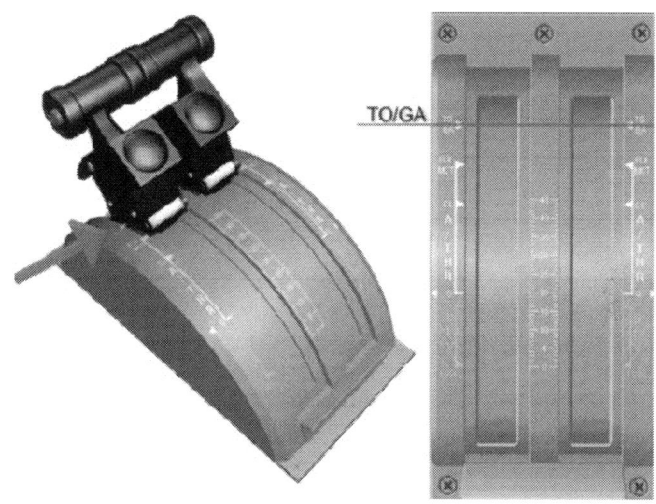

At any time during flight, pilots can disconnect both the autopilot system and the automatic thrust control system by simply pressing a button and taking manual control of the aircraft to continue flight manually.

Boeing 737 engine system

The aircraft is equipped with two CFM56-7 twin-rotor engines delivering a maximum thrust of 27,300 lbs.

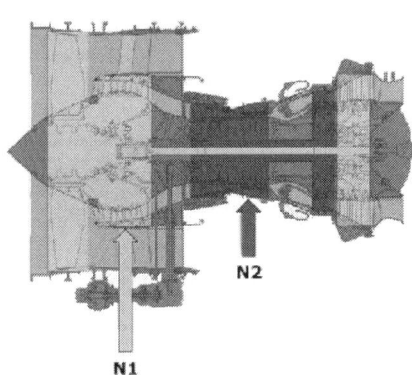

Each engine consists of several components that form the powerplant. Among the main components are two mechanically independent rotors (N1 and N2).

The first rotor, N1, consists of three working sections: the initial FAN composed of a series of wheel-shaped blades, a low-pressure compressor, and a low-pressure turbine.

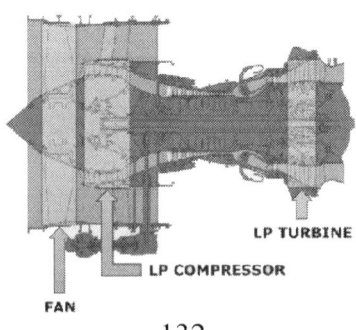

132

The second rotor, N2, consists of two sections: a high-pressure compressor and a high-pressure turbine.

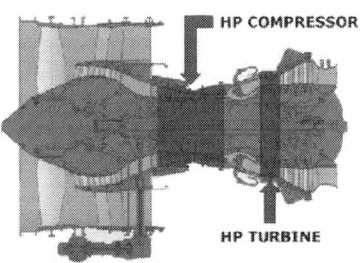

Each engine is controlled by a dual-channel electronic control called EEC (Electronic Engine Control). Its operation principle is based on information received from the AUTO THROTTLE system and the position of the thrust levers. With this information, the EEC regulates the amount of fuel reaching the engine through a hydromechanical unit called HMU (Hydro Mechanical Unit).

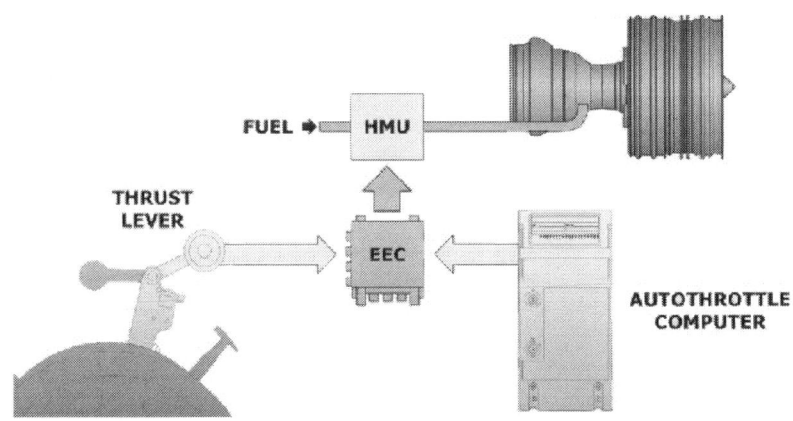

133

The operational principle of this engine is similar to other jet engines. It relies on the path of air entering the engine and passing through different stages to generate ignition and produce power.

Airflow enters the engine through the FAN at the front section. After passing through the FAN, the air takes two different paths. A portion of the air mass travels through the center of the engine, passing through the compressor section and the combustion chamber, where it mixes with fuel to ignite and produce thrust. This path is known as the primary airflow and contributes approximately 80% of the engine's power. The remaining airflow, known as secondary airflow, travels along the edges of the engine and is expelled at the rear.

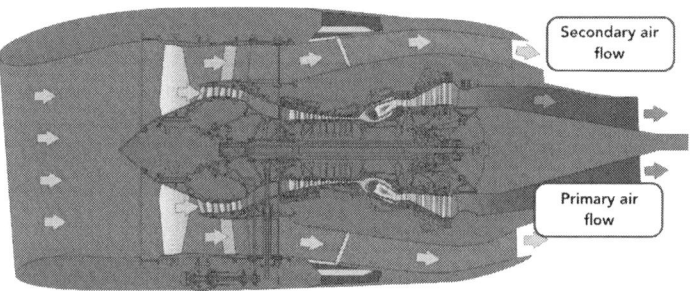

Part of the secondary airflow contributes to the operation of the thrust reverser system. This system involves opening the internal cavity of the engine to allow the secondary airflow to exit, generating reverse thrust opposite to the forward thrust, which reduces the landing roll or during a rejected takeoff (RTO).

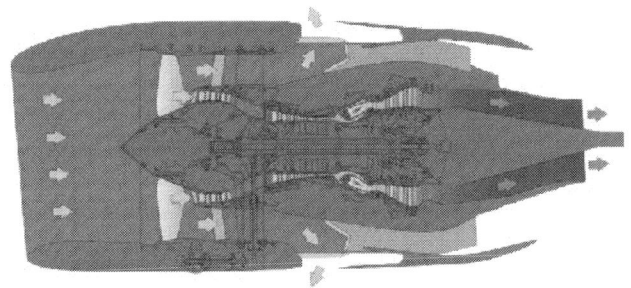

The engine's operational principle is based on a series of subsystems within the engine system. These subsystems work together to ensure successful operation. Within each N2 rotor are fuel pumps, oil pumps, hydraulic pumps, and an AC electrical generator, all housed in a section known as the "Gearbox". The proper functioning of these subsystems is essential for the correct operation of the engine.

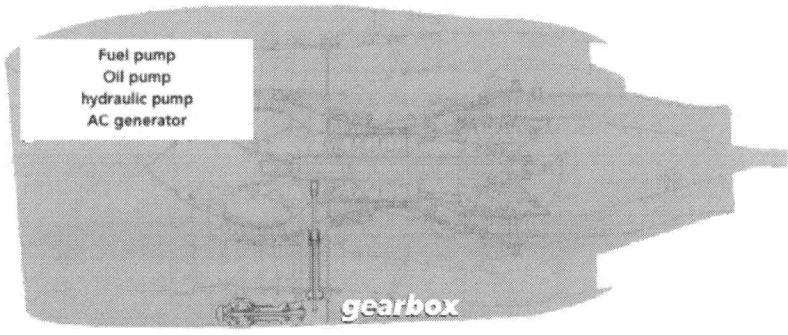

Fuel is transferred through a series of stages before reaching the engine's combustion chamber. This transfer is facilitated by the fuel pump, which maintains the necessary pressure in the fuel flow. Fuel from the tanks first passes through the primary pump, which

135

increases its pressure to allow it to pass through the heat exchangers before reaching the filter, where contaminants are removed. After exiting the filter, the fuel passes through the secondary pump to restore pressure lost in previous stages until it reaches the Hydromechanical Unit (HMU), which regulates the fuel flow under the control of the Electronic Engine Control (EEC).

The fuel then moves to the final stage, the fuel flow transmitter, before being delivered to the engine.

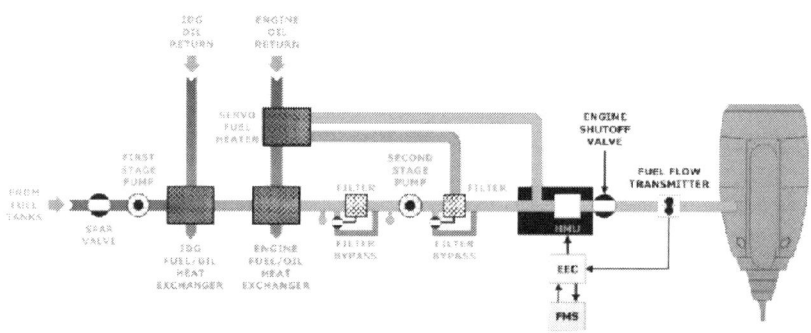

Located between the HMU and the fuel flow transmitter is the engine shutoff valve. When this valve is closed, fuel is prevented from reaching the combustion chamber, resulting in engine shutdown. In the cockpit, pilots monitor the fuel flow information provided by the Fuel Flow Transmitter on the Upper and Lower Display Units (DUs).

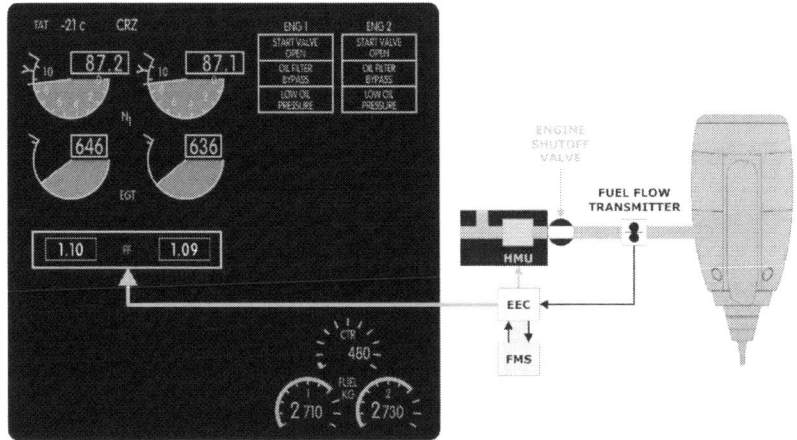

The oil pump functions similarly to the fuel pump, but the path of this fluid differs. The oil travels from its reservoir to the engine-driven oil pump. Here, it gains sufficient pressure to begin its journey through various sections, passing through a filter that removes contaminants, then through an oil temperature sensor, and continues its path until reaching the engine.

Within the system, the oil serves two purposes: cooling and lubricating the engine and its components. At the end of the cycle, the remaining oil returns to the system, passing through various stages until it reaches the starting point again to begin its cycle anew.

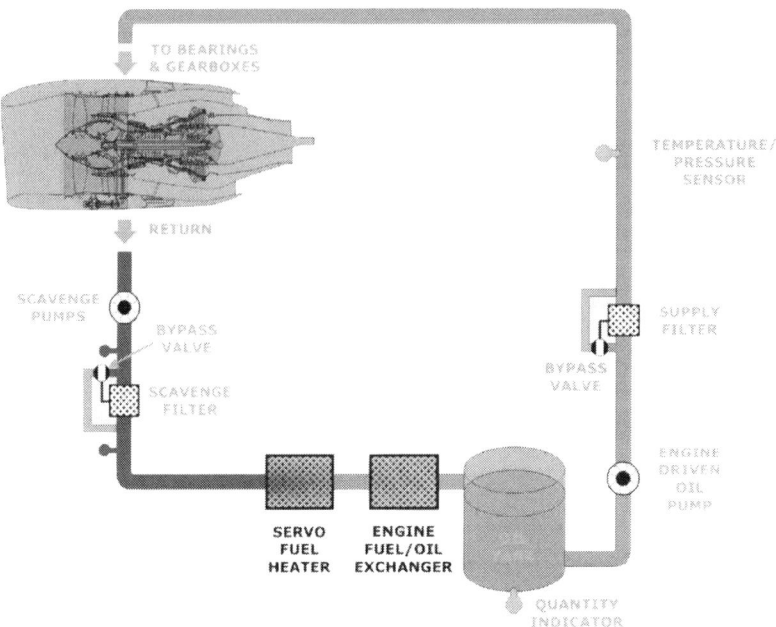

When starting the engine, the system draws bleed air from one of three possible sources: the already running engine, the APU, or an external pneumatic source.

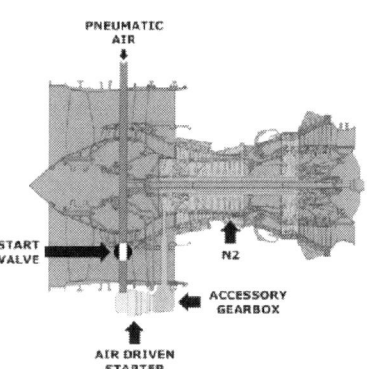

The start valve opens, allowing the airflow to enter. When N2 reaches 25%, the pilot moves the thrust levers to the IDLE position, opening the fuel valve and the HMU valve. This process initiates the next step, ignition.

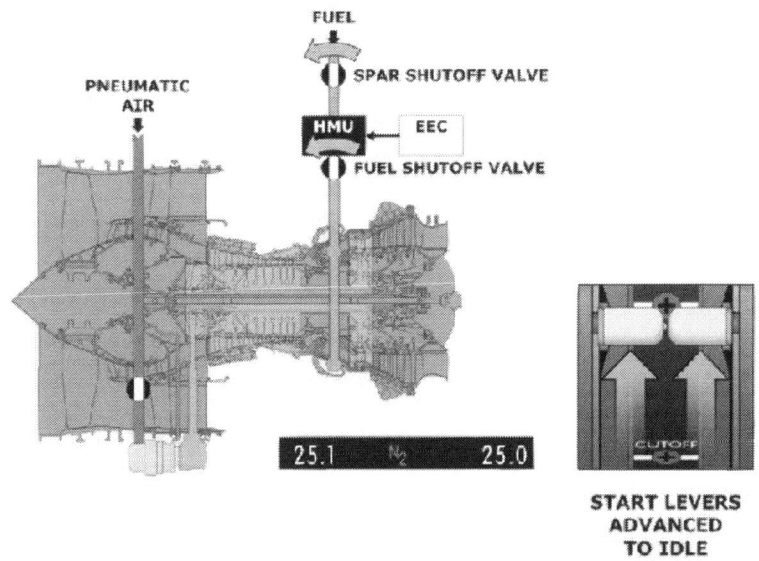

FUEL

SPAR SHUTOFF VALVE

PNEUMATIC
AIR

HMU ← EEC

FUEL SHUTOFF VALVE

25.1 N₂ 25.0

START LEVERS
ADVANCED
TO IDLE

From the Pedestal Panel, the pilot can control the engine power and the thrust reverser system, all from the throttle quadrant.

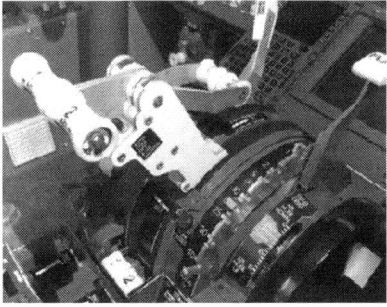

The throttle levers have a range of 58 degrees from the IDLE position to the maximum power position. During manual power operation, the pilot can adjust the power setting as necessary, but always within this operational range. The EEC system offers two power control modes: normal and alternate. In normal mode, the

EEC considers current flight conditions and air pressure demand to control the correct N1 value. In alternate mode, current flight conditions are not considered. These power control modes have their panel located on the rear overhead panel.

Within the same EEC panel are the two reverser indicators, one for each engine. The thrust reverser system reverses the thrust flow, generating a reduction in thrust during the landing roll or an aborted takeoff.

The reverser activation levers are located in front of each throttle lever corresponding to each engine. Their activation is rearward, in the same direction as power reduction.

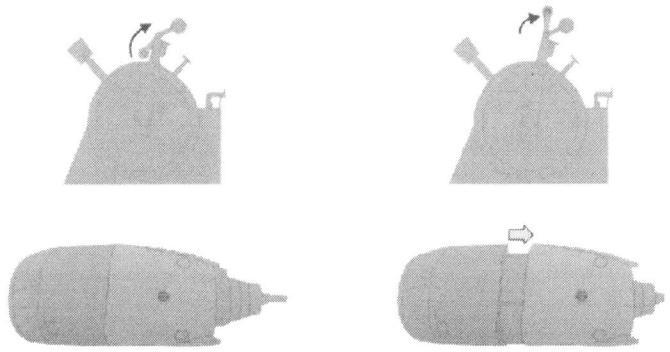

The activation of the system is subject to the fulfillment of three conditions. The aircraft must be below 10 feet AGL or on the ground, the battery switch must be ON, and the fire protection switches associated with each engine must be down or deactivated. Any deviation from these parameters would prevent the operation of the reversers.

As an additional safeguard, the thrust reverser lever locks in the IDLE REV position until the system has reached 60% deployment. This prevents the pilot from accidentally moving the levers forward.

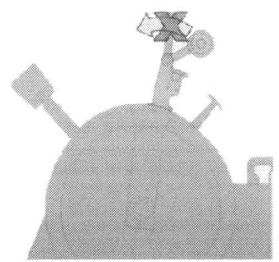

When the thrust reverser system is activated, the word "REV" appears on the upper display, just above the N1 indications for each engine, indicating that the system has been cngaged. While the reversers are in transit to full deployment, the word "REV" is displayed in amber. Once the reversers are fully deployed, the word "REV" is displayed in green.

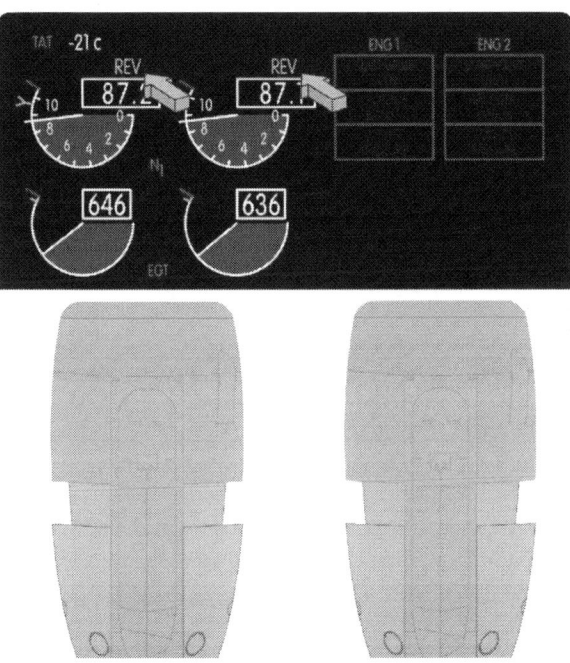

Chapter 5

Jet engine performance

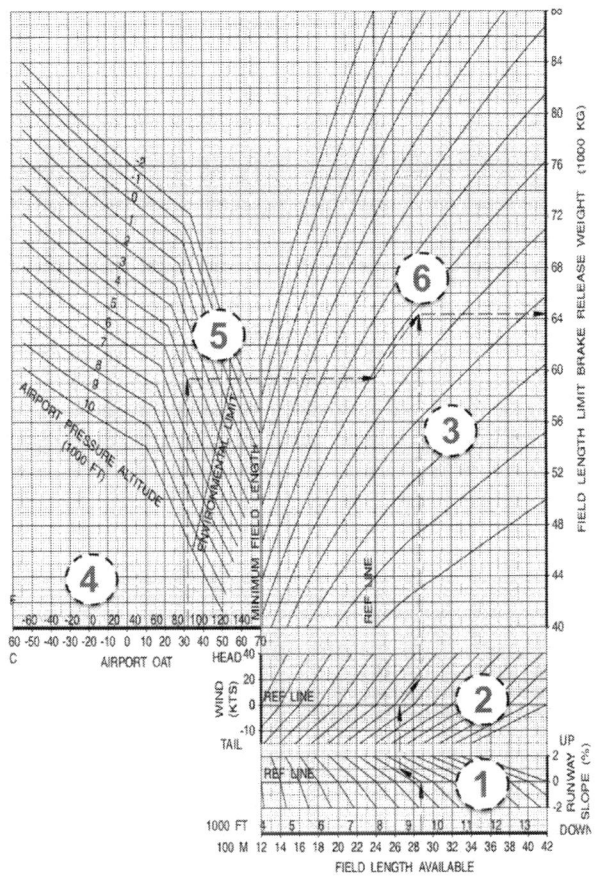

Takeoff weight limitations

For every maximum weight defined by the manufacturer, additional restrictions or limitations must be applied at takeoff. These are influenced by atmospheric conditions, obstacles in the takeoff path, and runway length. The latter is often the most common and restrictive factor. Consider an aircraft loaded with a TOW (Takeoff Weight) of 64,000 kg and a manufacturer-defined MTOW (Maximum Takeoff Weight) of 65,000 kg. Under normal conditions, this aircraft could take off without issues. However, if the aircraft is departing from an airport with high elevation, a runway slope, and a reduced runway length, the takeoff roll would need to be shorter and might not provide sufficient distance to achieve takeoff speed with 64,000 kg. Therefore, the aircraft's MTOW would be limited by runway length, resulting in a lower value than the specified 65,000 kg.

To determine this runway length-limited MTOW, the Takeoff Field Limit performance tables for a specific configuration are used. The following data is required for using these tables:

- Runway length and slope.
- Wind and temperature.
- Airport pressure altitude.

Let's explore the table and see, step by step, how to use it:

145

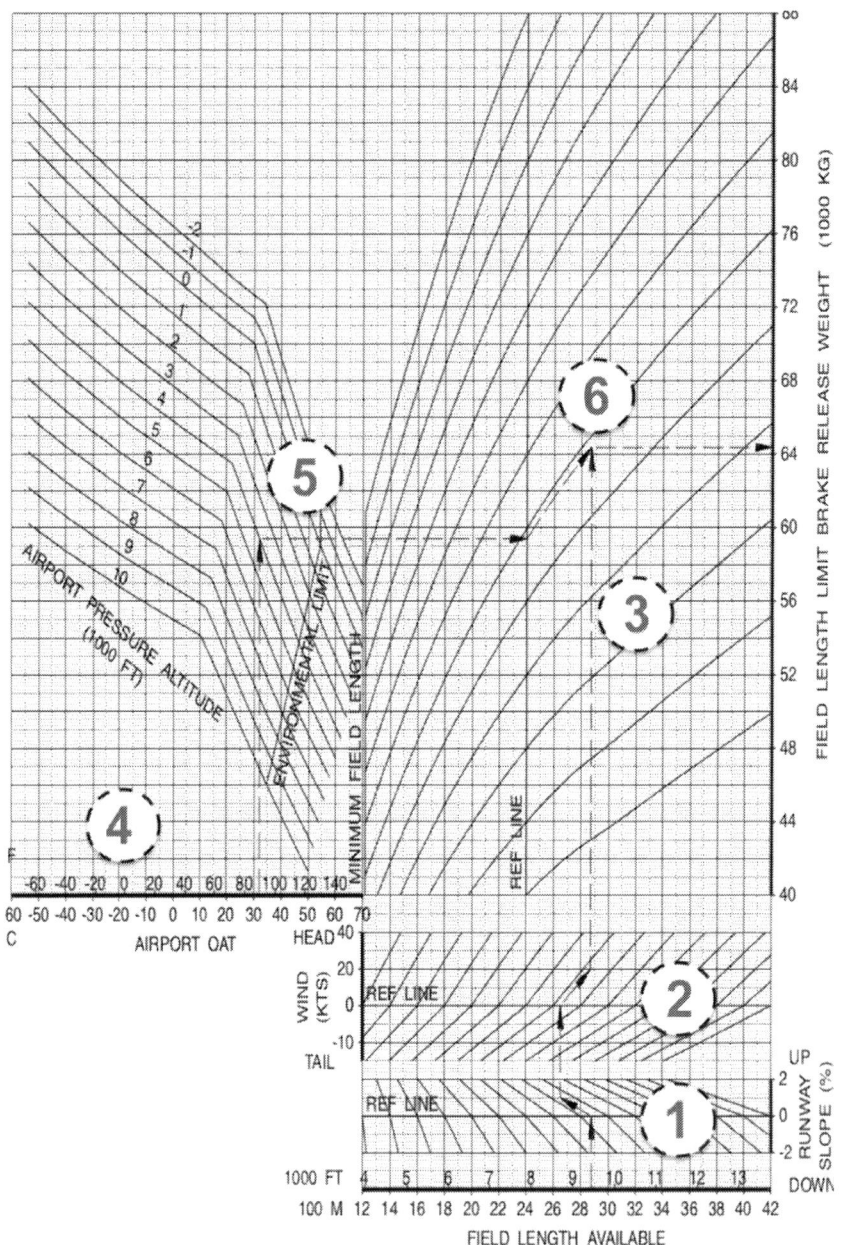

146

We will base our example on the conditions described in the table:

Runway length: 2840 meters.
Runway slope: 1.0% UP.
Wind: Headwind 20 KT.
Temperature: 32°C.
Airport pressure altitude: 4000 FT.

This is a double-entry table, meaning we need to enter data from two different sections, and finally, we will combine the results to obtain the desired value. Following the numerical sequence described in the example table, we will enter through section one corresponding to runway length and slope. Let's proceed:

Initially, we enter the table at the runway length value of 2840 meters (first point). From there, we move up to the reference line (REF LINE) of a 0% runway slope (second point), then continue parallel to the curved line until reaching our runway slope value of 1.0% UP (third point).

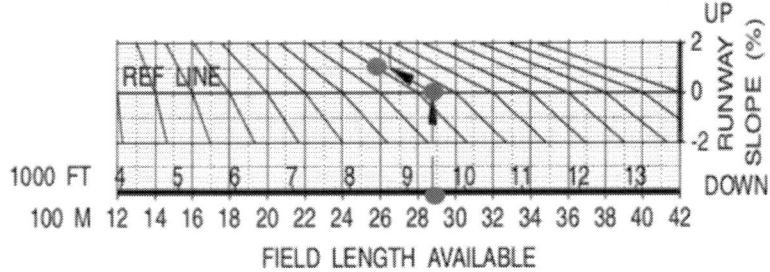

Continuing with the numerical sequence, we move to section two, where we need to input the wind data, starting from the endpoint of the previous step. From the point of a 1.0% UP runway slope, draw a straight line to the next REF LINE (zero wind) and from there, continue parallel to the curved line until reaching the corresponding wind intensity, in this case, 20 KT (final point).

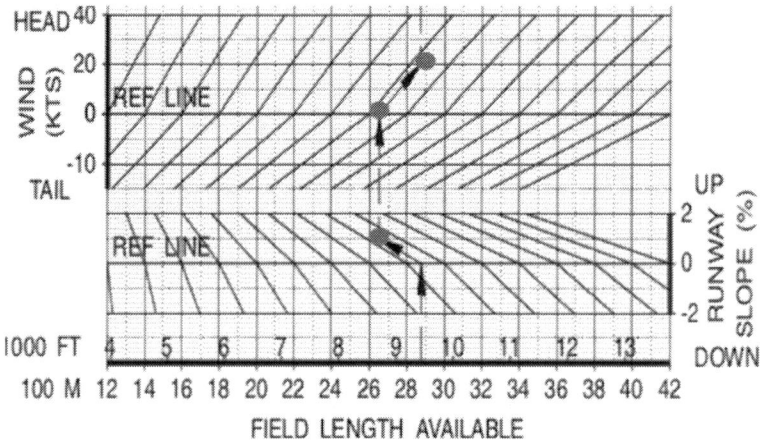

From the endpoint of the wind representation, draw a straight, parallel line to the next REF LINE but without a terminal point. This line will intersect with the results of the following calculations, as shown in point three of the table.

This completes the first section of data entry into the table. Now, it's time to re-enter the table using other variables such as temperature and airport pressure altitude.

148

We have completed the first section of data entry into the table. Now it's time to re-enter using other variables, such as temperature and airport pressure altitude. Following the numerical sequence, at point four, enter the temperature value, which in this case is 32°C, marked at the first point. From there, move vertically to reach point five in our sequence. Move straight up until reaching the airport pressure altitude, which is 4000 FT. Upon reaching the second point, draw a horizontal line to the right until you reach the next REF LINE, before intersecting with the line resulting from the first table entry.

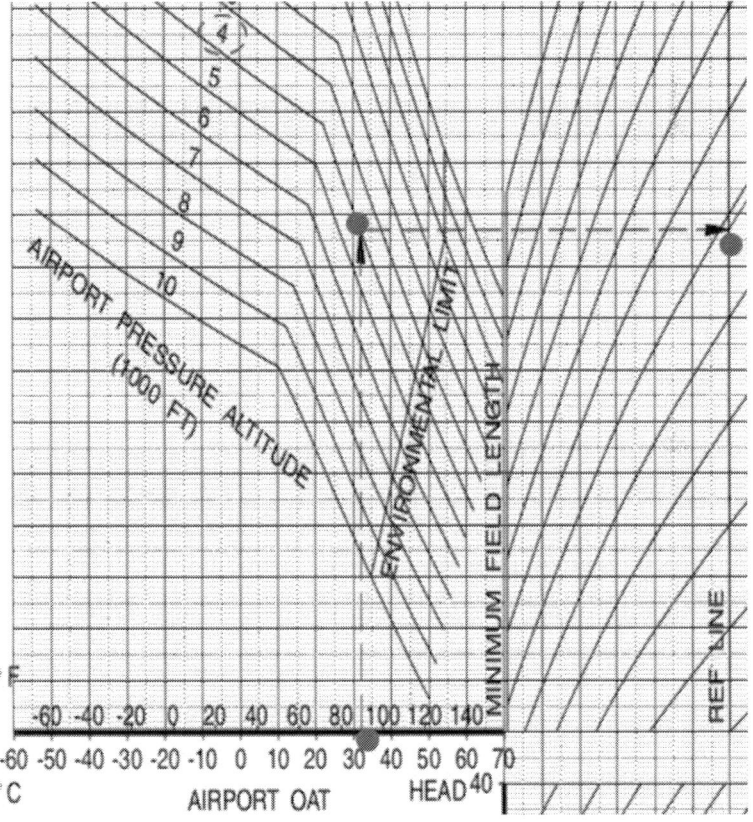

Finally, we reach point six of our numerical sequence. From the REF LINE of the previous step, continue parallel to the curved line until it intersects with the straight line from the first entry. From this intersection, draw a horizontal line to the right and read the value expressed in KG x 1000 to obtain the final result.

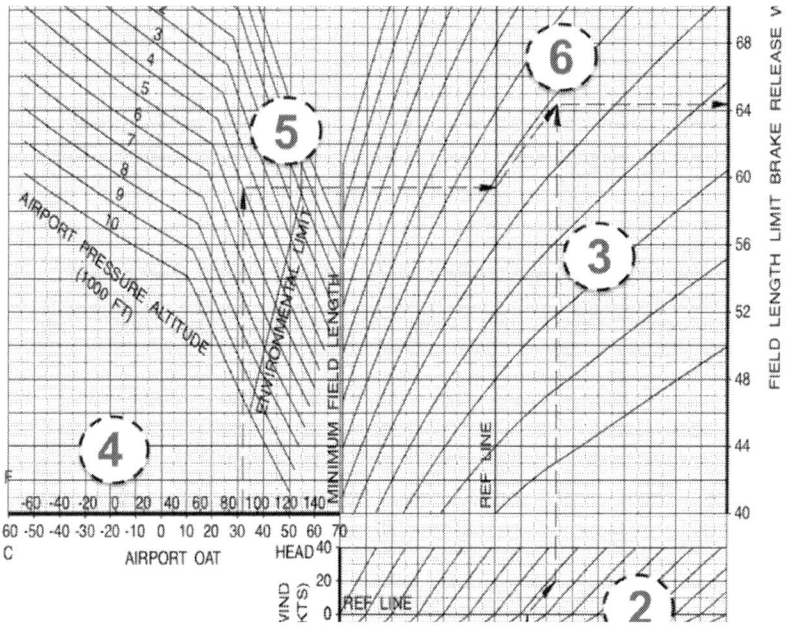

Final Result: The MTOW for this example is 64,500 KG. As we saw at the beginning, the manufacturer's MTOW was 65,000 KG, the current TOW was 64,000 KG, and the table indicates that, due to limitations, we could still load an additional 500 KG.

TOW Limited by obstacle

Continuing with TOW limitations, let's consider a common scenario for airports with obstacles in the runway path, the TOW limitation due to obstacle height.

This calculation is based on the principle that an aircraft with a higher weight requires a reduced climb gradient, which could prevent the aircraft from clearing an obstacle ahead. If the obstacle cannot be cleared, the MTOW must be corrected for obstacle height. Five variables are involved in this calculation:

- Obstacle height.
- Temperature.
- Pressure altitude.
- Wind conditions.
- Distance from the runway threshold to the obstacle.

For the following calculation, as with the previous ones, a specific configuration planned for takeoff is used. This configuration usually varies according to the flap position. For this chart study, we will consider the Flaps 1 configuration and divide the table into four sections, similar to the previous tables.

Let's begin by familiarizing ourselves with the complete table before proceeding through its different sections.

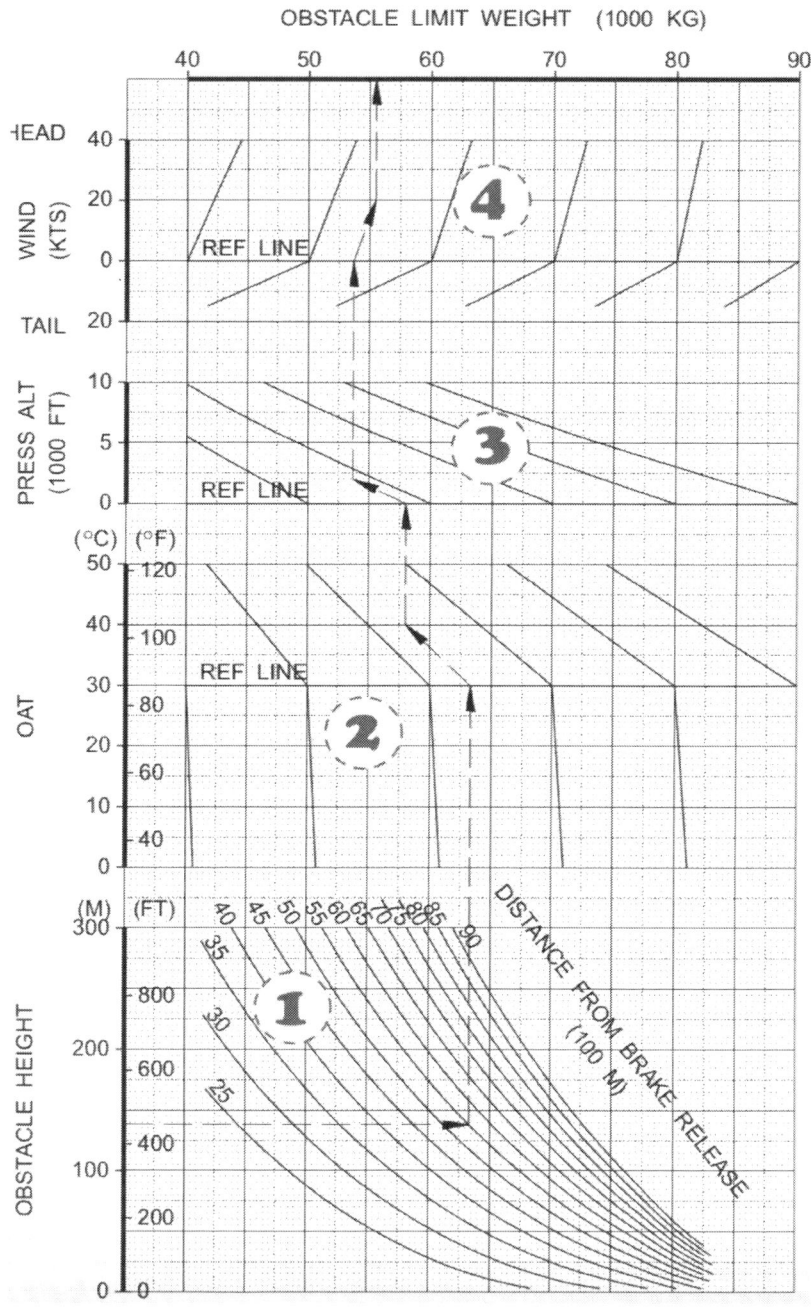

OBSTACLE LIMIT WEIGHT (1000 KG)

152

Before starting, let's consider an example and its five variables:

Obstacle height: 130 meters.

Temperature: 40°C.

Pressure altitude: 2500 FT.

Wind conditions: headwind 20 KT.

Distance to obstacle: 5500 meters.

We begin with a new numerical sequence at point one, where we enter the chart via the obstacle height, using the left margin scale, at the value of 130 meters (M). From there, draw a straight line to the curved line indicating the distance to the obstacle expressed in hundreds of meters. In our case, this is the line at 55. Upon reaching it, draw a vertical line upwards to begin the second step.

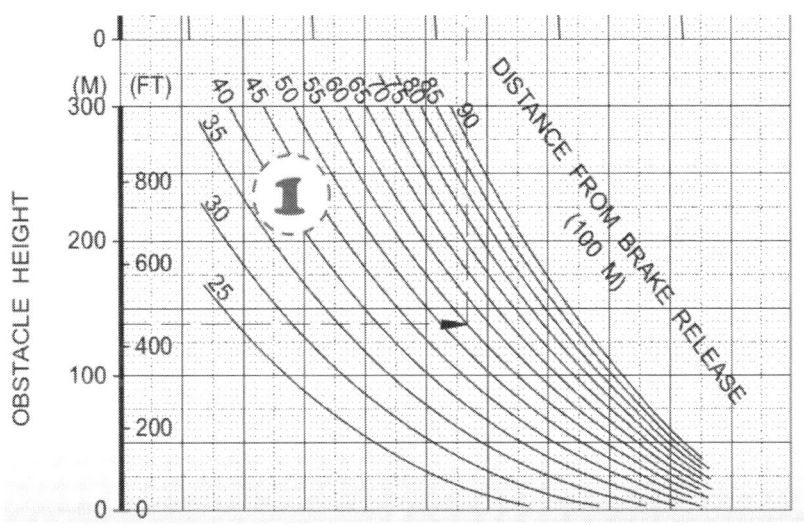

At the start of step two, continue the previously drawn straight line up to the REF LINE for the second variable, temperature. Upon reaching the REF LINE, proceed parallel to the diagonal reference line until the temperature of our example, 40°C.

From there, draw another vertical line up to the next REF LINE for the subsequent variable. Upon reaching this line, continue parallel to the diagonal line until our pressure altitude of 2500 FT. From here, again draw a vertical line upwards to the final variable in this table, the wind component, before reaching the final result.

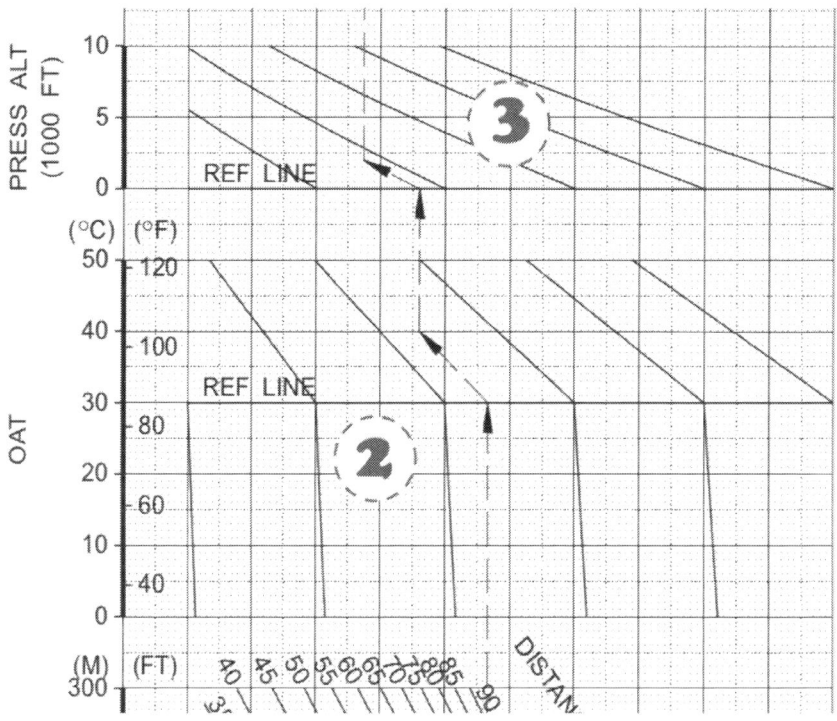

Finally, we reach point number four. We continue the trajectory of the straight line drawn at the end of the previous step until reaching the REF LINE of the last variable, the wind component. In our example, it is HEAD WIND 20KT. From the REF LINE, draw a line parallel to the diagonal reference until 20 KT, and from there, the last vertical line straight to the final value where we obtain the MTOW limited by obstacle height. In our particular case, based on the mentioned variables, the MTOW is 56000KG.

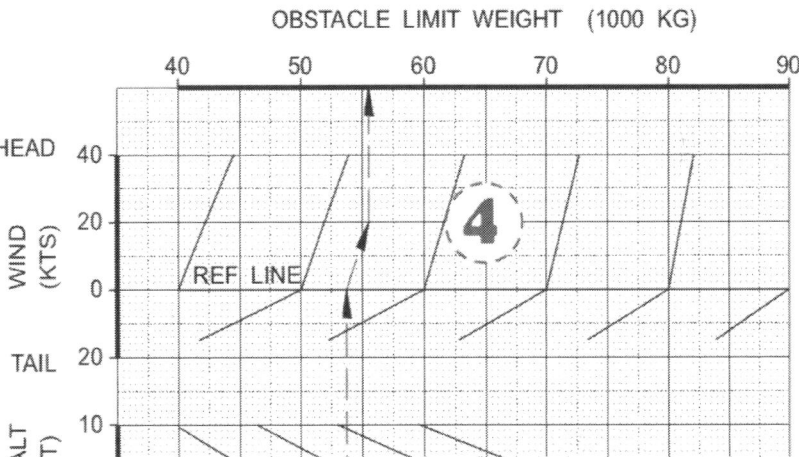

TOW Limited by climb gradient

Maintaining the same takeoff weight, using a lower flap setting results in a steeper climb gradient. This is due to lower flap settings causing reduced aerodynamic drag. Legally, a minimum climb gradient must be maintained to clear existing obstacles.

Therefore, using a lower flap setting allows for higher takeoff weights limited by climb gradients. We will base our example on takeoff with Flaps 1.

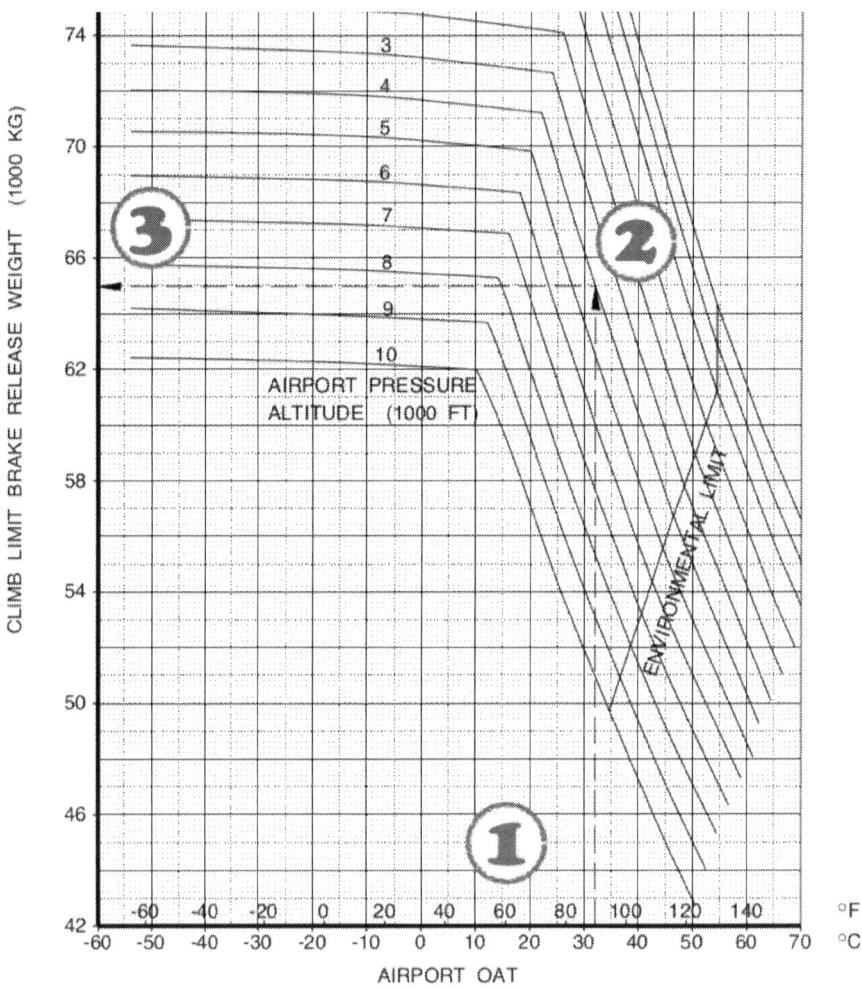

In this new table, we enter the airport temperature. For our example, it is 32°C, as indicated in point number one.

From there, draw a vertical line straight up to reach the REF LINE of the airport pressure altitude, which in our example is 4000FT, as indicated in point number two.

Once at the REF LINE of pressure altitude, draw a horizontal line straight to the left margin of the table where we can read the desired value, as indicated in point number three.

Based on the data entered in the table and for a specific flap setting, our takeoff weight limited by climb gradient will be 65000KG.

To better understand these limitations, let's compare it with a table for TOW limited by climb gradient but with a higher flap configuration.

In our previous result, the TOW limited by climb gradient with Flaps 1 was 65000KG. Now, let's look at the same table but for takeoff with Flaps 25.

Temperature: 32°C.
Pressure altitude: 4000FT.
Flap setting: 25.

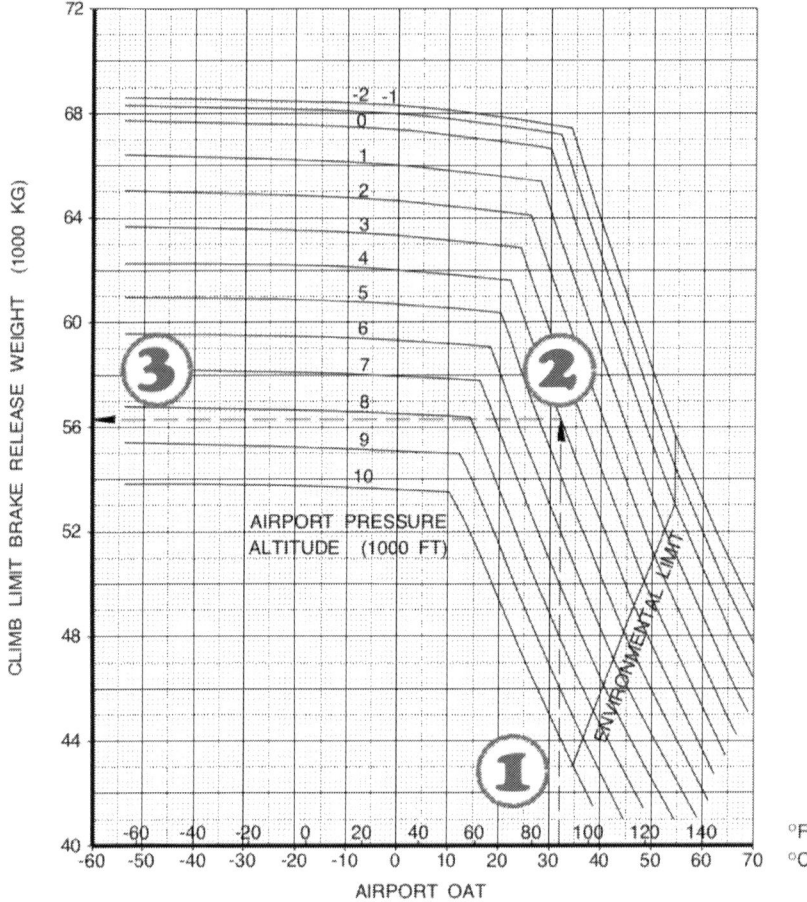

Following the numerical sequence, similar to the previous table, the calculated result shows a takeoff weight limited by climb gradient of 56500KG, compared to 65000KG. This means that under the same environmental conditions but with a different flap configuration, the takeoff weight could vary by 8500KG!

TOW limited by Improved climb

Approaching one of the final tables in the takeoff phase, we encounter the calculation of TOW for "Improved Climb Performance." Consider a specified TOW within limits, but imagine placing our aircraft on an extremely long runway, where the TORA (Takeoff Run Available) greatly exceeds what the aircraft requires for takeoff.

In such a scenario, the aircraft could utilize this extra runway length to increase its speed beyond what is strictly necessary, achieving a better climb rate. This principle or procedure leads us to the calculation of "Improved Climb," where the aircraft optimizes its takeoff speeds V1, VR, and V2 to achieve a higher climb gradient.

This method is employed to increase the maximum takeoff weight only when the limitation is due to climb performance. Typically used to enhance climb performance, it involves utilizing the excess runway available to increase takeoff speeds V1, VR, and V2 beyond their normal values. This allows for achieving a steeper climb gradient.

In this table, after completing the data entry, we will find two results. Towards the left of the table, we will locate the maximum TOW (Takeoff Weight) and towards the right, we will find the additional knots (KT) to add to each takeoff speed. Let's proceed:

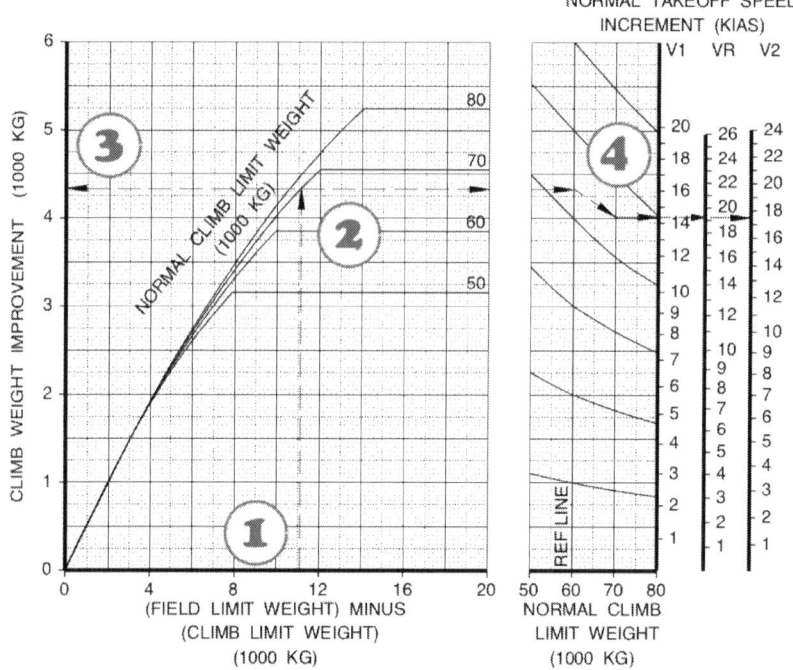

We will enter the chart using the difference between the TOW limited by runway length and the TOW limited by Climb, both values previously studied. In our example, the result of this subtraction is 11,000 kilograms, which we will enter at point number one. From there, we draw a straight line until we reach the value of TOW limited by Climb (point number two). Starting from this point, we will divide the path to obtain two results. We will draw a straight line towards the left edge (point number three) where we will find the additional kilograms that we could load onto our current TOW. Then, we will draw a line to the right towards the REF LINE (point four), and follow its curved line until we intersect with the value of TOW limited by Climb again. From here, we draw our straight line

160

towards the left margin and obtain the additional knots (KT) that we should add to our V1, VR, and V2 speeds to obtain the final values. Let's consider an example.

TOW limited by runway: 77000KG
TOW limited by climb: 63000KG
V_1: 130KT. V_R: 140KT. V_2:150KT.

Optimal Flight Level for Holding Patterns

Just like optimal cruising altitudes, there are also optimal levels or altitudes for flying in holding patterns, where aircraft performance achieves the best time-to-fuel consumption ratio.

This data is crucial because aircraft may depart with minimal required fuel for their planned flight and may not anticipate the need for air traffic control to require them to enter a holding pattern. In such situations, each aircraft should adjust its flight to the altitude that optimizes fuel consumption. Various tables are used for this purpose.

This is a table from Boeing for flying in holding patterns with flaps retracted. Let's imagine our aircraft currently weighs 70,000 KG and ATC instructs it to hold. To ensure minimal fuel consumption, we look up the aircraft weight in the table and find the column with the lowest fuel consumption value. To the left of this value, we find the column indicating the optimal altitude.

Holding Planning
Flaps Up

PRESSURE ALTITUDE (FT)	TOTAL FUEL FLOW (KG/HR)							
	WEIGHT (1000 KG)							
	85	80	75	70	65	60	55	50
41000							2110	1890
35000		3130	2800	2550	2330	2130	1940	1770
30000	3080	2860	2660	2470	2280	2090	1910	1750
25000	2980	2790	2600	2420	2230	2050	1890	1730
20000	2970	2780	2600	2430	2270	2110	1940	1780
15000	2990	2830	2630	2480	2310	2140	1980	1810
10000	3020	2840	2670	2500	2340	2180	2010	1850
5000	3030	2870	2700	2540	2370	2210	2050	1890
1500	3080	2910	2750	2590	2420	2260	2100	1950

Furthermore, this table serves another purpose: it allows us to determine the predicted fuel consumption when ATC mandates a hold at a specific flight level. For example, if ATC requires a hold at 30,000 FT and our aircraft weighs 65,000 KG, we can find the corresponding fuel consumption.

Let's now examine a different format from Airbus, which offers a similar table but with added values that may be of interest. Under similar conditions, Airbus provides fuel consumption values based on applied engine power, expressed in N1 values.

Holding Planning
Flaps Up

PRESSURE ALTITUDE (FT)	T(			
	85	80	75	70
41000				
35000		3130	2800	2550
30000	3080	2860	2660	2470
25000	2980	2790	2600	2420
20000	2970	2780	2600	2430
15000	2990	2830	2630	2480
10000	3020	2840	2670	2500
5000	3030	2870	2700	2540
1500	3080	2910	2750	2590

162

RACE TRACK HOLDING PATTERN - GREEN DOT SPEED

MAX. CRUISE THRUST LIMITS	ISA	N1 (%)
CLEAN CONFIGURATION	CG=33.0%	FF (KG/H/ENG)
NORMAL AIR CONDITIONING		
ANTI-ICING OFF		

WEIGHT (1000KG)	FL 15	FL 50	FL100	FL140	FL180	FL200	FL220	FL250
46	45.6 / 890	47.9 / 873	51.1 / 839	54.0 / 813	57.5 / 794	/ 789	60.6 / 787	63.5 / 784
48	46.5 / 926	48.9 / 908	52.1 / 871	55.1 / 844	58.4 / 828	58.9 / 823	61.7 / 821	64.7 / 818
50	47.4 / 962	49.8 / 940	53.0 / 901	56.2 / 876	59.4 / 861	60.0 / 859	62.8 / 855	65.8 / 851
52	48.3 / 997	50.6 / 971	53.9 / 931	57.3 / 908	60.3 / 896	61.0 / 892	63.9 / 889	66.7 / 884
54	49.2 / 1033	51.4 / 1002	54.9 / 963	58.3 / 942	61.3 / 931	62.0 / 926	65.0 / 924	67.7 / 916
56	50.1 / 1065	52.2 / 1033	55.8 / 994	59.1 / 975	62.2 / 964	63.0 / 960	66.1 / 955	68.6 / 949
58	50.8 / 1097	52.9 / 1063	56.8 / 1026	59.9 / 1008	63.2 / 997	64.1 / 994	66.9 / 988	69.5 / 982
60	51.5 / 1128	53.7 / 1094	57.7 / 1059	60.7 / 1043	64.1 / 1031	65.1 /	67.7 / 1021	70.4 / 1016
62	52.2 / 1158	54.5 / 1125	58.7 / 1092	61.6 / 1078	65.1 / 1065	65.9 / 1058	68.6 / 1054	71.2 / 1049
64	52.9 / 1189	55.3 / 1156	59.4 / 1126	62.4 / 1110	66.0 / 1097	67.7 / 1091	69.4 / 1087	72.1 / 1084
66	53.6 / 1219	56.1 / 1188	60.1 / 1159	63.2 / 1143	67.0 / 1129	68.6 / 1124	70.3 / 1120	72.9 / 1119
68	54.3 / 1250	56.9 / 1221	60.9 / 1193	64.1 / 1176	67.7 / 1162	69.3 / 1157	71.1 / 1154	73.7 / 1155
70	55.0 / 1282	57.8 / 1254	61.6 / 1228	64.9 / 1210	68.4 / 1195	70.1 / 1191	71.8 / 1188	74.6 / 1192
72	55.8 / 1314	58.6 / 1287	62.3 / 1261	65.7 / 1243	69.2 / 1228	70.8 / 1224	72.5 / 1223	75.4 / 1230
74	56.5 / 1347	59.4 / 1321	63.1 / 1294	66.6 / 1275	69.9 / 1262	71.6 / 1258	73.3 / 1258	76.1 / 1269
76	57.2 / 1380	60.2 / 1355	63.8 / 1327	67.4 / 1307	70.6 / 1296	72.3 / 1292	74.0 / 1295	76.9 / 1309
78	58.0 / 1413	60.8 / 1389	64.5 / 1360	68.2 / 1339	71.3 / 1330	73.0 / 1328	74.8 / 1332	77.6 / 1350

In this case, for holding at FL 200 (20,000 feet) with the aircraft weighing 64,000 KG, the fuel consumption corresponds to 1091 KG at an engine power indication of 67.7 N1.

Unlike Boeing's table, this one is slightly more precise and accurate in terms of fuel consumption as it defines this value based on the engine power applied.

Abnormal operations

As anticipated in earlier sections, additional data is often prepared for abnormal operations during the cruise phase, such as an engine failure or flying with landing gear extended due to a system malfunction. This information is typically discussed during a briefing in cruise phase on most flights, aiming to understand each aircraft's limitations in such scenarios.

Let's imagine that due to maintenance team instructions, the aircraft must fly with its landing gear fully extended. This situation will limit its ability to fly at higher altitudes and undoubtedly increase its fuel consumption. Let's look at the following table provided by Boeing for operations with extended landing gear. In this table of values, we can find the maximum altitude for flying with the landing gear extended. Imagine the aircraft weighs 65,000 KG and the outside temperature is ISA + 15˚C. Under these conditions, the maximum altitude to fly would be 23,500 FT.

WEIGHT (1000 KG)	PRESSURE		
	ISA + 10°C & BELOW	ISA + 15°C	ISA + 20°C
85	14600	11500	8500
80	17400	14600	11700
75	20300	17600	14900
70	22800	20500	17800
65	25400	23500	20900
60	27800	26300	24400
55	30200	29000	27300
50	32300	31300	30100
45	34500	33500	32400
40	36900	36000	34900

Let's proceed to Airbus again. In their manuals for the A320 fleet, they present a series of tables to consider in the event of an engine failure. Initially, they refer to the maximum operational altitude that an aircraft should fly over with one engine inoperative. To obtain this value, we refer to the "One Engine Out Max Altitude" table. Imagine our aircraft weighs 64,000 kg at the time of the engine failure and the temperature is ISA standard. In such a situation, we access the table from the bottom, using the weight value. From there, we draw a straight line until it intersects with the temperature line, and then draw another straight line to the left to read the desired value of "One Engine Out Max Altitude.

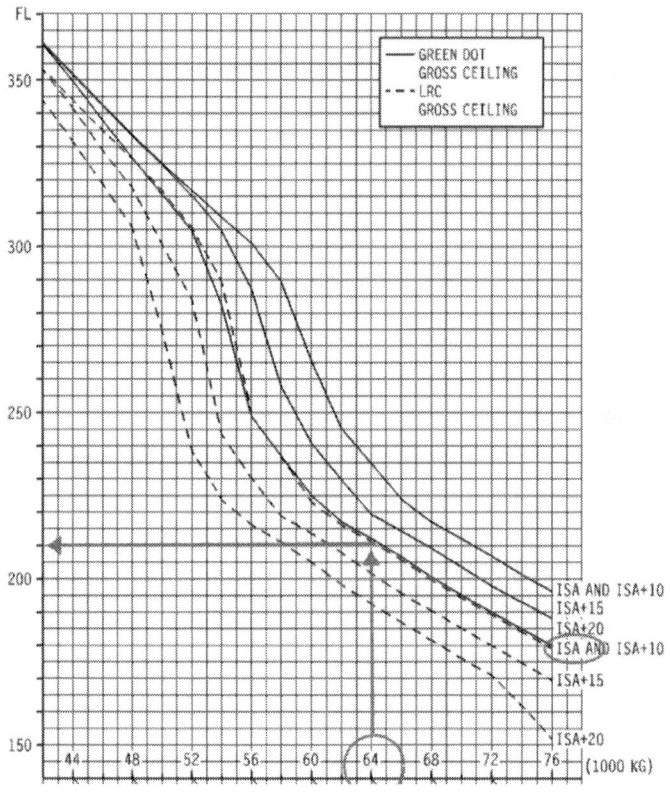

In our particular case, the obtained value is 21,000 feet (FL210). Now, once we have obtained the previous value, the next step is to obtain the optimal speed values and fuel consumptions at that altitude with one engine inoperative. For this purpose, there is a reference table. The following table represents 4 values for operations with one engine inoperative. We will obtain information on EPR, FUEL FLOW, MACH, and IAS. In our specific case, at FL210 and with 64,000 kg, we can consider that our aircraft, with one engine inoperative, flying at a speed of 267 knots, will have a fuel consumption of 2,272 kg. The values of EPR 1.418 refer to suggested power, and the value of MACH 0.595 refers to a second unit of speed.

LONG RANGE CRUISE - 1 ENGINE OUT						
MAX. CONTINUOUS THRUST LIMITS ... ISA PACK FLOW HI G=33.0% ANTI-ICING OFF			EPR FUEL FLOW (KG/H)		MACH IAS (KT)	
WEIGHT (1000KG)	FL100	FL150	FL190	FL210	FL230	FL250
50	1.151 .430 1811 237	1.236 .511 1968 258	1.267 .515 1792 240	1.316 .550 1841 247	1.344 .556 1777 239	1.393 .584 1801 241
52	1.158 .435 1879 240	1.240 .511 1987 257	1.292 .535 1907 250	1.327 .553 1881 248	1.363 .567 1855 244	1.412 .594 1874 246
54	1.170 .447 1983 247	1.245 .510 2011 257	1.312 .550 1999 256	1.338 .555 1925 249	1.385 .581 1947 251	1.431 .602 1942 249
56	1.183 .461 2098 255	1.250 .510 2040 257	1.323 .553 2044 258	1.355 .565 2001 253	1.404 .592 2024 255	1.440 .600 1963 248
58	1.226 .510 2373 283	1.260 .514 2095 259	1.333 .555 2086 259	1.374 .576 2086 259	1.417 .595 2071 257	1.444 .585 1952 242
60	1.233 .514 2415 285	1.270 .519 2156 261	1.346 .561 2145 262	1.394 .588 2174 264	1.420 .585 2065 252	1.452 .562 1935 232
62	1.236 .514 2434 285	1.294 .540 2287 272	1.362 .570 2225 266	1.410 .596 2248 268	1.426 .570 2055 246	
64	1.239 .513 2454 284	1.311 .552 2382 279	1.381 .582 2317 272	1.418 .595 2272 267	1.435 .544 2037 234	
66	1.243 .513 2476 284	1.322 .556 2432 281	1.397 .591 2399 277	1.421 .585 2264 263		

166

Cruise parameters

When referring to cruise segment parameters, we are discussing information regarding fuel consumption, speeds, distances, and power settings applied during this phase. These values are typically divided into two parts. On one hand, we have calculations for maximum speed (MAX SPD), and on the other hand, calculations to achieve the maximum possible range (LONG RAGE). Each manufacturer has designed specific tables for each of these options. The following table corresponds to MAX SPD calculations. Here, the manufacturer provides the table for a Mach 0.78 or M.78 speed as indicated in point one. Point two contains the information provided by the table. Points three and four outline the input data, where in our case, it's a weight of 58,000 KG at FL370. Let's see the results:

	CRUISE - M.78 ①					
MAX. CRUISE THRUST LIMITS NORMAL AIR CONDITIONING ANTI-ICING OFF				ISA+20 CG=33.0%	EPR KG/H/ENG NM/1000KG	MACH IAS (KT) TAS (KT) ②
WEIGHT (1000KG)	FL290	FL310	FL330	FL350	FL370 ④	FL390
50	1.220 .780 / 1352 302 / 178.0 481	1.227 .780 / 1245 289 / 191.8 477	1.235 .780 / 1151 277 / 205.7 474	1.250 .780 / 1081 264 / 217.2 470	1.269 .780 / 1028 2.. / 227.3 468	.780 / 986 241 / 237.1 468
52	1.222 .780 / 1357 302 / 177.4 481	1.229 .780 / 1251 289 / 190.8 477	1.240 .780 / 1165 277 / 203.3 474	1.256 .780 / 1099 264 / 213.8 470	1.278 .780 / 1046 252 / 223.5 468	1.310 .780 / 1006 241 / 232.3 468
54	1.224 .780 / 1363 302 / 176.6 481	1.232 .780 / 1259 289 / 189.7 477	1.245 .780 / 1181 277 / 200.5 474	1.263 .780 / 1117 264 / 210.2 470	1.288 .780 / 1065 252 / 219.6 468	1.324 .780 / 1033 241 / 226.2 468
56 ③	1.226 .780 / 1369 302 / 481	1.236 .780 / 1271 289 / 187.8 477	1.251 .780 / 1198 277 / 197.7 474	1.270 .780 / 1137 264 / 206.6 470	1.299 .780 / 1084 252 / 215.6 468	1.341 .780 / 1068 241 / 218.9 468
58	.780 / 302 / 174.9 481	1.240 .780 / 1286 289 / 185.6 477	1.256 .780 / 1216 277 / 194.8 474	1.279 .780 / 1155 26. / 203.4 470	1.311 .780 / 1106 252 / 211.4 468	
60	1.231 .780 / 1385 302 / 173.8 481	1.245 .780 / 1303 289 / 183.3 477	1.263 .780 / 1235 277 / 191.7 474	1.288 .780 / 1174 264 / 200.1 470	1.32. .780 / 1135 252 / 206.0 468	
62	1.235 .780 / 1397 302 / 172.3 481	1.250 .780 / 1320 289 / 180.9 477	1.269 .780 / 1255 277 / 188.7 474	1.298 .780 / 1193 264 / 196.8 470	1.341 .780 / 1170 252 / 199.8 468	

According to the table, flying at FL370 with a weight of 58,000 KG, we will obtain the following values:

EPR: 1.311 MACH: .78

KG/H/ENG: 1106

NM/1000KG: 211.4.

IAS: 252KT. TAS:468KT.

264	1084	252	1068	
470	215.6	468	218.9	
780	1.311	.780		
264	1106	252		
470	211.4	468		
780	1.325	.780		
264	1135	252		
470	206.0	468		

Your turn again! Let's look at the next cruise table at M.78 and obtain performance data for the following conditions:

1) Weight: 62000KG. FL: 350.
2) Weight: 52000KG. FL: 310.
3) Weight: 58000KG. FL: 390.

CRUISE - M.78												
MAX. CRUISE THRUST LIMITS NORMAL AIR CONDITIONING ANTI-ICING OFF								ISA CG=33.0%		EPR KG/H/ENG NM/1000KG		MACH IAS (KT) TAS (KT)
WEIGHT (1000KG)	FL290		FL310		FL330		FL350		FL370		FL390	
50	1.217	.780	1.223	.780	1.232	.780	1.246	.780	1.265	.780	1.293	.780
	1280	302	1177	289	1087	277	1019	264	969	252	930	241
	180.3	462	194.4	458	208.7	454	220.5	450	230.7	447	240.5	447
52	1.219	.780	1.226	.780	1.237	.780	1.253	.780	1.274	.780	1.305	.780
	1284	302	1183	289	1099	277	1036	264	987	252	949	241
	179.7	462	193.4	458	206.3	454	217.1	450	226.6	447	235.7	447
54	1.221	.780	1.229	.780	1.242	.780	1.259	.780	1.284	.780	1.320	.780
	1290	302	1190	289	1115	277	1053	264	1005	252	973	241
	178.9	462	192.2	458	203.5	454	213.4	450	222.6	447	229.8	447
56	1.223	.780	1.233	.780	1.248	.780	1.266	.780	1.295	.780	1.337	.780
	1296	302	1200	289	1131	277	1072	264	1023	252	1006	241
	176.1	462	190.6	458	200.6	454	209.7	450	218.6	447	222.3	447
58	1.225	.780	1.237	.780	1.253	.780	1.275	.780	1.307	.780	1.355	.780
	1302	302	1215	289	1148	277	1090	264	1044	252	1041	241
	177.2	462	188.4	458	197.6	454	206.3	450	214.3	447	214.9	447
60	1.228	.780	1.242	.780	1.260	.780	1.284	.780	1.321	.780	1.376	.780
	1311	302	1230	289	1166	277	1108	264	1070	252	1078	241
	176.1	462	186.0	458	194.6	454	202.9	450	209.1	447	207.4	447
62	1.232	.780	1.247	.780	1.266	.780	1.294	.780	1.337	.780	1.399	.780
	1321	302	1247	289	1185	277	1127	264	1103	252	1120	241
	174.7	462	183.5	458	191.5	454	199.5	450	202.9	447	199.8	447

Time and fuel consumption

Currently, flight time and fuel consumption calculations during flight are provided by automated flight systems known as Flight Management Computers (FMC). These systems provide the crew with a variety of information, among the most valuable being times and consumptions at various waypoints or at the destination.

However, let's consider a scenario where the FMCs of each aircraft are out of service; this is where the old tables come into play to perform these calculations and obtain similar results, albeit perhaps slightly less precise but quite accurate.

Each manufacturer provides crews with a series of tables that determine various calculations. In this particular case, we will examine tables for "Trip Fuel and Time" calculations. For this purpose, the manufacturer must consider the different possible situations during a cruise flight, and for each scenario, they should prepare a specific table.

Next, we will examine a specific table for the cruise phase in LONG RANGE CRUISE configuration, flying at .78 Mach with a planned distance range between 200NM and 1000NM.

Long Range Cruise Trip Fuel and Time
200 to 1000 NM
Based on 280/.78 climb and .78/280/250 descent

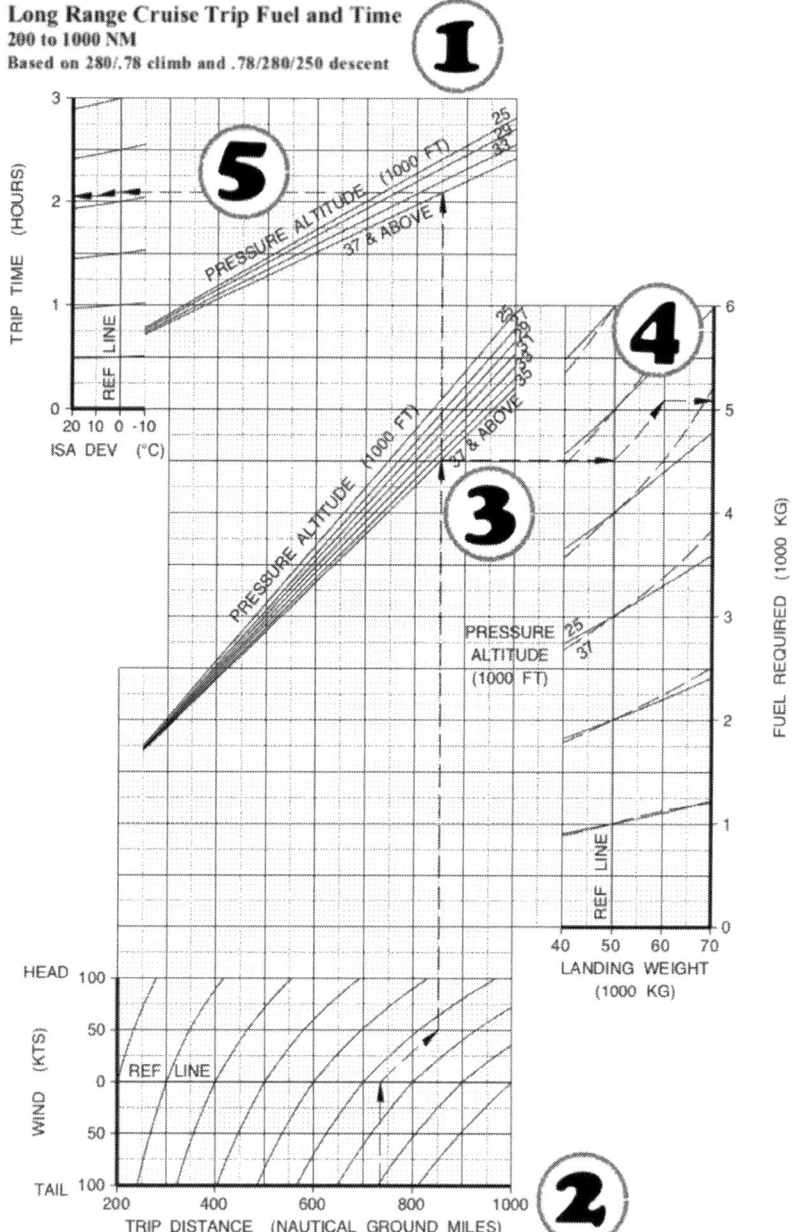

As we can see in point number one, there is a description of the table and its respective limitation. In this case, it is a specific table for calculations at speeds of .78 Mach and distances ranging from 200NM to 1000NM.

Long Range Cruise Trip Fuel and Time
200 to 1000 NM
Based on 280/.78 climb and .78/280/250 descent

Moving on to point number two, we will enter the table using the values of the distances to be covered and the current wind. In our example, the aircraft needs to cover a distance of 730NM, with a headwind condition of 50 knots at its flight level (FL).

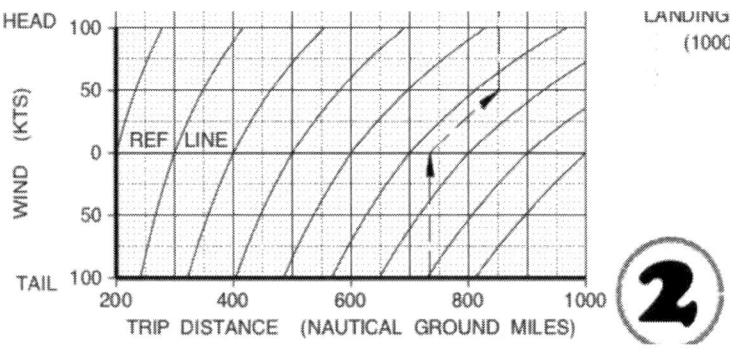

From the distance, we draw a straight line to the wind REF LINE, and from there, a curved line parallel to the reference up to the wind speed (50KT).

From here, we move on to point number three. We draw a vertical straight line to the line corresponding to our flight's pressure altitude.

171

In our particular case, the flight is conducted at FL370, which is 37,000 feet. At this point, the table is divided into two sections, and each line or arrow will follow a different path. On one hand, the reference that goes to the right will seek the value of the fuel required to cover the indicated distance. On the other hand, the reference that goes up and then to the left will seek the value indicating the flight time to cover the desired distance. Let's see:

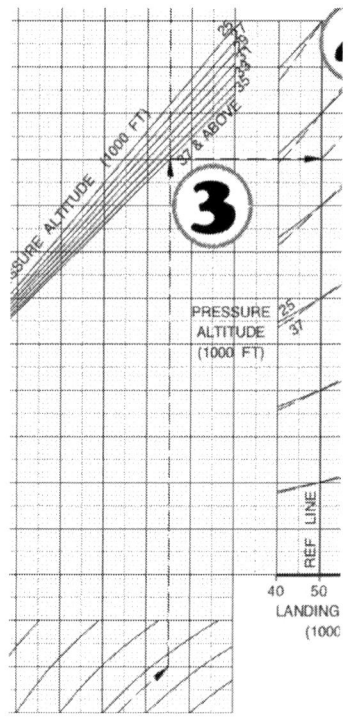

From point number three, we draw a straight line to the right until we reach the REF LINE, then a curved line parallel to the reference to the end, where we read the sought value. In this case, the fuel required to fly the 730NM will be approximately 5100 kilograms. Let's save this value for later and move on to point number five, starting from point number three where the sections were divided.

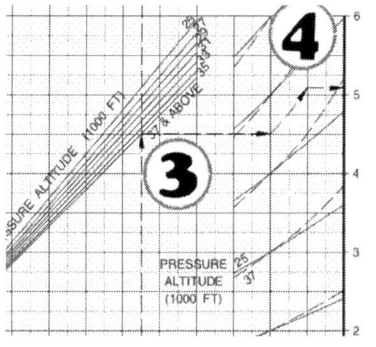

172

Let's search for the next value, the flight time. From point number three, we continue with a straight line similar to the previous one, extending it to the 37000 feet pressure altitude line. From there, we draw a straight line to the temperature REF LINE and then continue with a curved line parallel to the reference until the left margin where we will read the final value. In our particular case, it will be approximately 2 hours.

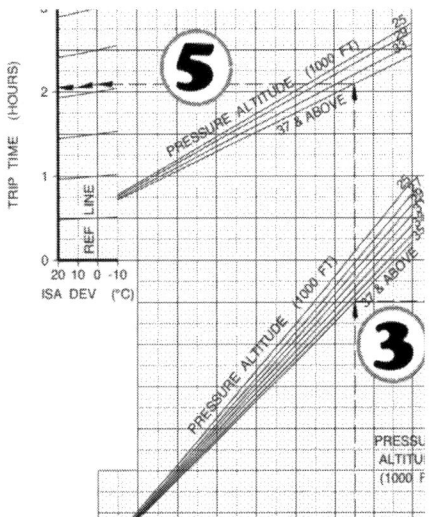

Summarizing the previous steps, we have obtained results indicating that for flying a distance of 730 NM under the mentioned conditions, approximately 5000 kg of fuel would be required, and the flight time to cover such distance would be around 2 hours. As mentioned earlier, these results are often quite precise but not exact, as the tables are meticulously designed, though variations can occur depending on the pencil strokes and correct line guidance.

Landing distance

One of the most important values to know before landing is the Landing Distance (LD), but we must not confuse this value with

173

the Landing Distance Available (LDA), which is a fixed value for each runway, as seen at the beginning of this manual.

To determine LD, several variables must be considered:

- Aircraft configuration.
- Runway condition, dry or wet.
- Reported braking action of the asphalt surface.
- Brake system configuration.

In addition to the value obtained from these variables, adjustments should be made for secondary factors such as:

- Weight.
- Altitude.
- Wind.
- Slope.
- Temperature.

Let's look at a detailed example of an LD calculation table from Boeing for its 737 fleet:

BRAKING CONFIGURATION	REFERENCE DISTANCE 60000 KG LANDING WEIGHT	WEIGHT ADJUSTMENT PER 5000 KG ABOVE/BELOW 60000 KG	ALTITUDE ADJ PER 1000 FT STD/HIGH*	WIND ADJ PER 10 KTS HEAD WIND	WIND ADJ PER 10 KTS TAIL WIND	SLOPE ADJ PER 1% DOWN HILL	SLOPE ADJ PER 1% UP HILL	TEMP ADJ PER 10°C ABOVE ISA	TEMP ADJ PER 10°C BELOW ISA
Runway DRY Flap 15 (LANDING DISTANCE AND ADJUSTMENTS (M))									
MAX MANUAL	945	70/-55	20/25	-35	115	10	-10	20	-20
MAX AUTO	1225	70/-70	25/35	-45	145	5	-5	30	-30
AUTOBRAKE 3	1745	120/-115	45/60	-75	250	5	-5	45	-45
AUTOBRAKE 2	2240	170/-170	65/85	-100	340	35	-40	65	-65
AUTOBRAKE 1				-115	400	65	-70	70	-70

Good Reported Braking Action

BRAKING CONFIGURATION									
MAX MANUAL	1310	85/-80	35/45	-55	200	30	-25	30	-30
MAX AUTO	1445	90/-85	35/45	-60	205	30	-25	35	-35
AUTOBRAKE 3	1750	120/-115	45/60	-75	250	10	-10	45	-45
AUTOBRAKE 2	2240	170/-170	65/85	-100	340	35	-40	65	-65

Medium Reported Braking Action

BRAKING CONFIGURATION									
MAX MANUAL	1800	135/-130	55/70	-90	330	75	-60	45	-45
MAX AUTO	1885	135/-130	55/75	-90	330	80	-60	45	-50
AUTOBRAKE 3	1935	140/-135	55/75	-95	340	60	-40	50	-50
AUTOBRAKE 2	2290	175/-170	70/90	-110	385	60	-55	65	-65

Poor Reported Braking Action

BRAKING CONFIGURATION									
MAX MANUAL	2360	220/-180	75/105	-135	520	190	-125	65	-65
MAX AUTO	2450	190/-180	75/105	-135	520	190	-125	65	-65
AUTOBRAKE 3	2450	190/-180	75/105	-135	520	185	-120	65	-65
AUTOBRAKE 2	2545	200/-195	80/110	-145	540	170	-110	70	-70

Starting with point number one, we find information regarding the planned braking configuration for landing and the reported asphalt braking action by the airport. In most heavy aircraft, the braking configuration is typically automatic with three or four different positions, or manual with a single possible option, depending on the intensity with which the pilot applies the brakes. Regarding the asphalt braking action, it is often described in three categories: good, medium, and poor, although this information may not always be reported by the ATIS or air traffic control. In such cases, the assumption would be the first section, where no braking action detail is provided.

To continue with each point, let's assume there is no indication of braking action and we are only looking at the top part of the table.

At point number two, we find the reference landing distance for a standard weight of 60,000 kilograms. This indication serves as a reference point to which we add adjustments for additional weight and other variables we will discuss here.

Runway DRY Flap 15 ①	LANDING DISTANCE AND ADJUSTMENTS (M)									
	REFERENCE DISTANCE	WEIGHT ADJUSTMENT	ALTITUDE ADJ	WIND ADJ PER 10 KTS		SLOPE ADJ PER 1%		TEMP ADJ PER 10°C		
BRAKING CONFIGURATION	60000 KG LANDING WEIGHT	PER 5000 KG ABOVE/BELOW 60000 KG	PER 1000 FT STD/HIGH*	HEAD WIND	TAIL WIND	DOWN HILL	UP HILL	ABOVE ISA	BELOW ISA
MAX MANUAL	945	70/-55	20/25	-35	115	10	-10	20	-20
MAX AUTO	1225	70/-70	25/35	-45	145	5	-5	30	-30
AUTOBRAKE 3	1745	120/-115	45/60	-75	250	5	-5	45	-45
AUTOBRAKE 2	2240	170/-170	65/85	-100	340	35	-40	65	-65
AUTOBRAKE 1		② ③	④	-115 ⑤	400	65 ⑥	-70	70 ⑦	-70

In point number three, adjustments begin, specifically adjustments based on weight. According to the table, adjustments should be made for every 5000 kilograms above or below 60,000 kilograms, adding or subtracting the specified value accordingly. Let's consider an example: For a manual braking configuration, the reference landing distance (LD) is 945 meters. Assuming our estimated weight is 65,000 kilograms, we would refer to the first row of weight adjustments which shows 70/-55. Since our weight is above 60,000 kilograms, we add 70 meters to the 945 meters, resulting in a corrected landing distance of 1015 meters. If our weight had been 55,000 kilograms instead, we would subtract 55 meters from the initial 945 meters, resulting in a corrected landing distance of 890 meters.

176

In point number four, we will follow a similar process, but here we will only add the value indicated in the column to the previous result. It's important to note that each column's value should be added sequentially to the result from the previous column. Considering the previous result of 1015 meters, let's assume the runway is at an elevation of 2000 feet above sea level. According to the table, we should add 40 meters to the previous value of 1015 meters, as 20 meters are added for every 1000 feet of elevation. Therefore, the final corrected landing distance will be 1055 meters.

Runway DRY Flap 15 ①	LANDING DISTANCE AND ADJUSTMENTS (M)								
	REFERENCE DISTANCE	WEIGHT ADJUSTMENT	ALTITUDE ADJ	WIND ADJ PER 10 KTS		SLOPE ADJ PER 1%		TEMP ADJ PER 10°C	
BRAKING CONFIGURATION	60000 KG LANDING WEIGHT	PER 5000 KG ABOVE/BELOW 60000 KG	PER 1000 FT STD/HIGH*	HEAD WIND	TAIL WIND	DOWN HILL	UP HILL	ABOVE ISA	BELOW ISA
MAX MANUAL	945	70/-55	20/25	-35	115	10	-10	20	-20
MAX AUTO	1225	70/-70	25/35	-45	145	5	-5	30	-30
AUTOBRAKE 3	1745	120/-115	45/60	-75	250	5	-5	45	-45
AUTOBRAKE 2	2240	170/-170	65/85	-100	340	35	-40	65	-65
AUTOBRAKE 1	2 ②	2 ③ 5	④	-115 ⑤	400	65 ⑥	-70	70 ⑦	-70

Upon reaching point number five, we proceed with the correction for wind component where we will add or subtract from our previous value of 1055 meters. Let's consider a headwind component of 20 knots. According to the HEAD WIND section, we should subtract 35 meters for every 10 knots of headwind. Therefore, in our case, we need to subtract 70 meters from the previous value of 1055 meters to obtain the corrected value adjusted for the wind component. The result will be 985 meters, which should be noted for the calculation in the next column.

177

Similar to the previous point, point number six is divided into two columns, one for downhill runway slope and the other for uphill runway slope. Let's imagine for our calculation that we know the runway has a slope of -2%. In this case, we should add 20 meters to our previous value of 985 meters, resulting in a partial corrected value of 1005 meters, adjusted for runway slope.

Runway DRY Flap 15 **(1)**	LANDING DISTANCE AND ADJUSTMENTS (M)								
	REFERENCE DISTANCE	WEIGHT ADJUSTMENT	ALTITUDE ADJ	WIND ADJ PER 10 KTS		SLOPE ADJ PER 1%		TEMP ADJ PER 10°C	
BRAKING CONFIGURATION	60000 KG LANDING WEIGHT	PER 5000 KG ABOVE/BELOW 60000 KG	PER 1000 FT STD/HIGH*	HEAD WIND	TAIL WIND	DOWN HILL	UP HILL	ABOVE ISA	BELOW ISA
MAX MANUAL	945	70/-55	20/25	-35	115	10	-10	20	-20
MAX AUTO	1225	70/-70	25/35	-45	145	5	-5	30	-30
AUTOBRAKE 3	1745	120/-115	45/60	-75	250	5	-5	45	-45
AUTOBRAKE 2	2240	170/-170	65/85	-100	340	35	-40	65	-65
AUTOBRAKE 1	**(2)**	**(3)**	**(4)**	-115 **(5)**	400	65 **(6)**	-70	70 **(7)**	-70

Finally, we arrive at point number seven, the correction for ambient temperature. Let's imagine that at our destination, the temperature is 20°C. This corresponds to the column ABOVE ISA as it is above 15°C, and we should add the first value of 20 meters to the 1005 meters obtained previously, resulting in a total of 1025 meters. As the final result for a landing on a dry runway, with Flaps 15, in manual braking configuration, weighing 65000KG, at a runway elevation of 2000FT, with a headwind component of 20KT, a runway slope of -2%, and a temperature of 20°C, we obtain a corrected LD of 1025 meters!

Let's continue with another example, this time using a different table from the manufacturer Airbus for their A320 fleet

Understanding the nuances between Boeing and Airbus calculations is notable, particularly Airbus's methodology of adjusting landing distances by applying varying percentages to a reference value, whereas Boeing adjusts by adding or subtracting specific meters. Let's proceed to enter the table with the current landing weight as specified in point number one. Let's assume it's 62,000 kilograms. Moving to point number two, we need to determine whether the runway is dry or wet. For a dry runway, the distance would be 840 meters, and for a wet runway, it would be 1,180 meters. However, in this case, we must consider the specific conditions of the wet runway.

1	ACTUAL LANDING DISTANCE (METERS)									
	WEIGHT (1000 KG)	46	50	54	58	62	66	70	74	78
2	DRY	700	730	770	800	840	910	990	1080	1170
	WET	920	980	1040	1110	1180	1240	1320	1390	1460
RUNWAY CONDITION / 3 COVERED WITH	6.3 MM (1/4INCH) WATER	1220	1300	1380	1480	1590	1700	1810	1930	2020
	12.7 MM (1/2INCH) WATER	1190	1260	1340	1430	1530	1630	1730	1840	1930
	6.3 MM (1/4INCH) SLUSH	1180	1260	1340	1420	1500	1580	1670	1770	1860
	12.7 MM (1/2INCH) SLUSH	1150	1220	1300	1370	1450	1530	1610	1700	1780
	COMPACTED SNOW	1190	1270	1340	1410	1480	1550	1620	1700	1750
	ICE	2570	2690	2820	2950	3090	3230	3370	3510	3620

CORRECTIONS

4	CORRECTION ON ACTUAL LANDING DISTANCE							
	dry runway	wet runway	runway covered with					
			1/4 inch water	1/2 inch water	1/4 inch slush	1/2 inch slush	compacted snow	ice
per 1000 ft above SL	+ 3 %	+ 3 %	+ 4 %	+ 4 %	+ 5 %	+ 4 %	+ 3 %	+ 4 %
per 10 kt headwind	No correction for headwind due to wind correction on approach speed							
per 10 kt tailwind	+ 18 %	+ 21 %	+ 23 %	+ 21 %	+ 22 %	+ 20 %	+ 18 %	+ 31 %
forward C.G.	+ 2 %	+ 3 %	+ 3 %	+ 3 %	+ 3 %	+ 3 %	+ 3 %	+ 3 %

Let's consider that the runway, in addition to being wet, is covered with 6mm of water, resulting in a partial LD of 1590 meters. Moving on to point number four, corrections need to be made. In this case, Airbus proposes adjusting the partial landing distance according to the following variables: runway elevation; headwind or tailwind; center of gravity (CG) position; and inoperative reversers.

CORRECTIONS

4		CORRECTION ON ACTUAL LANDING DISTANCE						
	dry runway	wet runway	runway covered with					
			1/4 inch water	1/2 inch water	1/4 inch slush	1/2 inch slush	compacted snow	ice
per 1000 ft above SL	+ 3 %	+ 3 %	+ 4 %	+ 4 %	+ 5 %	+ 4 %	+ 3 %	+ 4 %
per 10 kt headwind	No correction for headwind due to wind correction on approach speed							
per 10 kt tailwind	+ 18 %	+ 21 %	+ 23 %	+ 21 %	+ 22 %	+ 20 %	+ 18 %	+ 31 %
forward C.G.	+ 2 %	+ 3 %	+ 3 %	+ 3 %	+ 3 %	+ 3 %	+ 3 %	+ 3 %
2 reversers operative	–3 %	–8 %	–10 %	–10 %	–9 %	–8 %	–8 %	–24 %

Let's return to our example, where our current landing distance is 1590 meters. Now, imagine that the runway is at an elevation of 2000 feet above sea level, which would require an additional 8% correction. This means we should add 127 meters to the 1590 meters, resulting in a partial total of 1717 meters.

Next, imagine that we have a tailwind component of 10 knots, and the aircraft's reversers are operational. For this scenario, we would add 23% for the tailwind, which is 395 meters to 1717, resulting in 2112 meters. Finally, we should subtract 10% for having operational reversers, which means subtracting 211 from 2112. As a final result, our landing distance corrected for these variables will be 1901 meters.

Bibliography related

- Motores aeronáuticos (Conforti)

- Instrumentos del avión (Conforti)

- Introducción a 737 (Conforti)

- Introducción a 320 (Conforti)

- Performance (Conforti)

- The turbine pilot (Brown & Holt)

181

Made in the USA
Columbia, SC
31 August 2025

e2e23bdd-2f87-46ed-89ad-e1317e3de3d4R02